The Matthew Experiment

How Matthew's Gospel can help you know Jesus better

by
Andrew Page

ISBN 978-3-95776-069-2

© by Andrew Page, 2018

All rights reserved. No part of this book may be reproduced in any form
or by any means without permission in writing from the publisher,
VTR Publications, Gogolstr. 33, 90475 Nürnberg, Germany,
info@vtr-online.com, http://www.vtr-online.com.

Scripture quotations taken from The Holy Bible,
New International Version (Anglicised edition).
© 1979, 1984, 2011 by Biblica (formerly International Bible Society).
Used by permission of Hodder & Stoughton Publishers, a Hachette UK company.
All rights reserved.
'NIV' is a registered trademark of Biblica (formerly International Bible Society).
UK trademark number 1448790.

Author photo on the back cover:
(c) Roger Eldridge Photography, www.eldridgephotos.com

Cover design: Chris Allcock

Contents

Acknowledgements 5

My Introduction: Invitation to an Experiment 7
Matthew's Introduction (Matthew 1:1 – 2:23) 13
    Section One: The Teacher (Matthew 3:1 – 7:29) 23
    Section Two: The Lord (Matthew 8:1 – 11:1) 50
    Section Three: The Enemy (Matthew 11:2 – 13:53) 71
    Section Four: The Son (Matthew 13:54 – 19:2) 90
    Section Five: The Judge (Matthew 19:3 – 26:2) 115
    Section Six: The Lover (Matthew 26:3 – 28:20) 147
My Conclusion: The Experiment goes on 164

Appendix 1: Questions about Matthew's Gospel 167
Appendix 2: The Mirror Links in Section Six 169
Appendix 3: The Matthew Experiment in a Home Group 170
Appendix 4: The Structure of Matthew's Gospel 177

Acknowledgements

I am very grateful to Thomas Mayer at VTR for agreeing to publish this book. And Chris Allcock has, once again, done a great job with the section drawings and the cover design.

A number of people read the manuscript and gave me their comments and suggestions, so I am glad to thank them here: Paul Allcock, David Bacon, Graham Ball, Bethany Devonish, Victoria Hibbs, Biddy Taylor and Wolfgang Widmann.

I have many friends who have prayed for me in the writing of this book: I owe them a huge debt. Many of them (but not all) are part of Above Bar Church, Southampton: I would be a lesser person without my church family.

Matthew's Gospel is the first of the Gospels I remember getting very excited about, more than thirty years ago. Since then Mark's Gospel and John's Gospel have taken centre stage, but in the last year I have started meeting Jesus in Matthew's Gospel as I have learnt to meditate my way though this wonderful book.

I am praying that many other people will experience the same thing.

To God be the glory!

Andrew Page
andrew@themarkdrama.com

My Introduction: Invitation to an Experiment

This is a book about two things at once.

First, it's about learning the Gospel of Matthew. I don't think Matthew originally wrote his book to be read but to be listened to: few people in the first century could have expected to own a copy for themselves. Matthew wrote it so people could memorize it. Not word for word, but bit by bit – so they could get to know Jesus better and tell the story to others.

So, second, this is a book about rediscovering Jesus. You may already know Matthew's Gospel very well, or you may just be starting out: but as we spend time together in his book the aim will be that we will get to admire, love and enjoy Jesus more. If that's what you want, you're in the right place.

So that's what the experiment is about: learning the Gospel so we can get to know Jesus better. I hope you will try it out for yourself.

Please take time to read the rest of this introduction. It won't take you long, but it will help you get the maximum out of *The Matthew Experiment*.

The Structure of Matthew's Gospel

After an introduction, which is the whole of the first two chapters, Matthew has divided the story he wants to tell into six main sections.

Each section consists of a narrative part (what Jesus does) and a teaching part (what Jesus says). And at the end of every teaching part Matthew signals the end of the section (and so the beginning of a new one) by using the expression *When Jesus had finished...* (see chapter 7:28; 11:1; 13:53; 19:1; 26:1).

Look, for example, at Section Two, which runs from Matthew 8:1 to 11:1. Here is the structure as I see it:

Narrative (8:1 – 9:38)

A. Who Jesus loves (8:1-17)
B. Two warnings for disciples (8:18-22)
C. Where Jesus is Lord (8:23 – 9:8)
D. Two stories for disciples (9:9-17)
E. What Jesus does (9:18-34)
F. Two facts for disciples (9:35-38)

Teaching (10:1 – 11:1)

A. Mission: its authority (1-4)
B. Mission: its description (5-15)
C. Mission: its opposition (16-25)
D. Mission: its secret (26-42)

There are five things to notice about this structure:

1. The narrative part reveals something about Jesus

In this case it shows his power and authority, so that already the question is being asked *Who is this man?*

You will notice that Jesus does do some teaching in this narrative part, but these are brief interludes rather than the sustained teaching we encounter in the teaching part of the section.

2. The teaching part develops what the narrative part reveals

Having reached out to people in need in the narrative part of Section Two, Jesus now sends his disciples out to do the same.

All the sections have a teaching part which makes explicit what we have seen in the narrative part.

3. The whole section has a main theme

The theme of Section Two is The Lord. In the narrative part we witness the effortless authority of Jesus, while in the teaching part he sends his disciples out, giving them authority to do what he has done.

And every one of the six sections has its own theme which focuses on Jesus.

4. I have added sub-headings to both parts of the section

Let me explain what I mean. Some of the sections cover a number of chapters in Matthew's Gospel, which means some of the parts are rather long.

So, in order to help us grasp their message I have added sub-headings. For example, here are my sub-headings for the narrative part of Section Two:

A. Who Jesus loves (8:1-17)
    1. He heals a leper (1-4)
    2. He heals a centurion's servant (5-13)
    3. He heals Peter's mother-in-law (14-15)

B. Two warnings for disciples (8:18-22)
1. A man who claims too much (18-20)
2. A man who offers too little (21-22)

C. Where Jesus is Lord (8:23 – 9:8)
1. He rules nature (23-27)
2. He crushes evil (28-34)
3. He forgives sin (9:1-8)

D. Two stories for disciples (9:9-17)
1. Jesus calls Matthew and eats with sinners (9-13)
2. Jesus predicts a radical break with Judaism (14-17)

E. What Jesus does (9:18-34)
1. He gives life (18-26)
2. He opens eyes (27-31)
3. He loosens tongues (32-34)

F. Two facts for disciples (9:35-38)
1. What Jesus feels (35-36)
2. What Jesus wants (37-38)

And I have done the same thing for the teaching part of the section.

If you don't like my sub-headings I have no problem with that: feel free to find some which work better for you. But sub-headings, especially in the longer parts of the Gospel, will help us to get hold of the meaning.

(For the complete outline of my structure of Matthew's Gospel, see Appendix 4.)

5. The section can easily be learnt by heart

This is not about learning every word, but simply the order of the events (with the sub-headings) in the section. I have tested this: most people can do this in 10 minutes.

This is true despite the fact that the structure of each section is different. But it is always true that each section has a narrative part, followed by a teaching part, followed by the phrase *When Jesus had finished...*

And that the order of the events in any section can be committed to memory.

But why should I learn Matthew's Gospel by heart?

That's a great question. But there are some very good reasons:

I. Because the Bible is the word of God it has remarkable power. We often forget this. In Psalm 119:11 David says to God: *I have hidden your word in my heart that I might not sin against you.*

II. Because Matthew has written his Gospel to make this easy. Even though the structure of each section is different, you will notice how easy it is to learn them all. My guess is that the Holy Spirit led Matthew to write this way because he wants us to have his word in our hearts.

III. Because learning the Gospel in this way makes it possible to do Bible study in the shower without getting your Bible wet! Of course I normally have my Bible with me when I am doing Bible study, but sometimes it's brilliant to meditate on the Bible just using your memory. So as you are walking down the road you can tell yourself the Gospel events and begin talking to Jesus about what you are remembering.

IV. Because I would love you to experience what I have experienced. I fell in love with Matthew's Gospel back in 1984, before focusing much more on the Gospels of Mark and then John. But more recently I have rediscovered this Gospel and have been able to meditate my way through the book. The Holy Spirit has used this to help me experience Jesus more. And that makes me want to share this with others.

How to use this book

This book is like a basic commentary, but one you can read through rather than just using for reference. As we look at each of the six main sections of Matthew there'll be an introduction called *Enjoying the View*: this provides the structure and the main theme of the section.

Next comes *Unpacking the Content*. Here I look at each part of the section in turn, explaining the message and then teaching through that part of Matthew's Gospel.

Then I make some suggestions as to how you could memorize the section (this is called *Learning the Gospel*). Most people aren't used to learning by heart, but it really is worth it. And remember we're not talking about learning every word but the order of events (with the sub-headings) in the section. As I mentioned above, most people can do this in 10 minutes (and look at some simple learning tips in the box on page 22).

One good way of getting the learning done is to team up with a friend. You agree to both read through, say, Section One and learn the order of events. Then you meet up to go for a walk or have a coffee, and re-tell the section together (see My Conclusion, point 3, page 165, for more details). Doing this with a friend will help you to do the learning rather than just skip it!

The last part is called *Meeting the Lord.* This is a reminder of the reason we are doing all this: we want to rediscover Jesus. As you talk to the Lord about what you remember from what you have been reading, you will start knowing, admiring and loving him more.

Please don't read *The Matthew Experiment* too quickly! You might want to take a week over each of the six sections, so that you have time to let what you are reading sink in. If you and a friend are both trying the experiment, you might meet up once a week to tell one another the stories and to talk about Jesus.

Thank you for reading my introduction; now it's time to read Matthew's.

I am praying that everyone who reads this book will enjoy Matthew's Gospel and enjoy meeting Jesus. The Matthew experiment starts now…

Matthew's Introduction
Matthew 1:1 – 2:23

It seems natural to conclude that Matthew's introduction to his Gospel covers the first two chapters: there is a gap of nearly 30 years between the end of chapter 2 and the start of chapter 3.

Unlike Mark, Matthew is determined to go back to Jesus' birth and childhood. But he does more than that: with his genealogy at the beginning of the Gospel he is telling us that the Jesus story actually started many centuries before his birth.

So this introduction is much more than the introduction to a Gospel: it is an introduction to Jesus. Matthew wants us to know that Jesus is more than the long-awaited Jewish Messiah.

He is God himself. And he deserves our worship.

Enjoying the View

A. Jesus: the climax of history (1:1-17)
   1. He's the son of Abraham (1-2)
   2. He's the son of David (1-17)
   3. He's the Jewish Messiah (1,16,17)

B. Jesus: a supernatural birth (1:18-25)
   1. Matthew says it (18)
   2. The angel says it (19-21)
   3. Scripture says it (22-23)

C. Jesus: worshipped by Gentiles (2:1-12)
   1. They follow a star (1-2)
   2. They learn from Scripture (3-8)
   3. They worship Jesus (9-12)

D. Jesus: protected by God (2:13-23)
   1. The first dream (13-18)
   2. The second dream (19-22a)
   3. The third dream (22b-23)

It would be good to take time to read through Matthew's Introduction. For many of us most of what we read will be very familiar: let's be praying that God will open our eyes to see Jesus more clearly.

Because that's what the experiment is about.

Unpacking the Content

A. Jesus: the climax of history (1:1-17)

In a western culture we are not too excited by genealogies! But Matthew starts his Gospel like this because he wants to tell us three things about Jesus: he is *the Messiah, the son of David, the son of Abraham* (1b).

1. – He's the son of Abraham (1-2)

Matthew spells it out: *Abraham was the father of Isaac, Isaac the father of Jacob…* (2a). Of course Abraham had ancestors too. But by beginning with Abraham, Matthew is making it very clear that Jesus is related to the father of Judaism.

When calling Abraham, God had promised *I will make you into a great nation, and I will bless you* (Gen 12:2a). Matthew is pointing us here to an important conclusion: Jesus is part – and perhaps the fulfilment – of that blessing.

2. – He's the son of David (1-17)

In his genealogy Matthew is giving us the line of royal succession (as opposed to Luke, who gives us the physical line from Adam to Joseph – see Luke chapter 3:23-38).

So why the royal line?

Well, it isn't to say that everything leading up to the birth of Jesus was faultless. Matthew includes four women of what we might call irregular marital status: *Tamar* (3), *Rahab* (5), *Ruth* (5) and *Uriah's wife* (6).

It is not unknown to include women in a Jewish genealogy. But Matthew wants to tell us that even the royal line came from some fairly insecure beginnings.

But there is something the list points to alongside this: Jesus is the son of David.

Matthew divides the genealogy into three parts (2-6a, 6b-11, 12-16). The ends of the first two parts highlight two turning-points in the history of Israel: David becoming king (see 6) and the loss of that kingship at the Babylonian exile (see 11).

Now, at the end of the third part of the genealogy, Jesus the son of David comes, and the kingship reaches its appointed goal.

Jesus is the climax of history.

This is made all the clearer by what Matthew writes at the end of his genealogy: *Thus there were fourteen generations in all from Abraham to David, fourteen from David to the exile to Babylon, and fourteen from the exile to the Messiah* (17).

This is significant because the numerical values of the Hebrew letters of the name David add up to fourteen (D=4, W=6, D=4). This is the explanation for Matthew's insistence on fourteen generations in each part of the genealogy (although in fact the first and last parts contain only thirteen, and Matthew misses out three generations in the middle part in order to make the pattern of fourteens work).

But the message is clear: Jesus is the son of David.

And that very expression will have made first-century Jewish readers prick up their ears. Everyone knew that the saviour God had promised would be a descendant of King David, so much so that the phrase *son of David* was another way of referring to the Messiah.

Which brings us to the third thing Matthew wants to tell us about Jesus.

3. – He's the Jewish Messiah (1,16,17)

Matthew begins his book with *Jesus the Messiah* (1), and he uses the title again at the end of the genealogy: *...and Jacob the father of Joseph, the husband of Mary, and Mary was the mother of Jesus who is called the Messiah* (16).

First-century Jewish expectations of the Messiah focused on a political king who would defeat the occupying Romans and restore independence to Israel.

But Matthew is going to make it clear that he understands *Messiah* very differently: we will see this as we continue to read through his Gospel.

And verse 17, which summarizes the genealogy, shows unmistakeably that Matthew sees *the Messiah* as the climax of history: he is the one the whole of history has been leading up to.

So how did he come into our world?

B. Jesus: a supernatural birth (1:18-25)

The main emphasis in this paragraph is that God, not Joseph, is the father of Jesus. Matthew has already more than hinted at this at the end of the genealogy we have just looked at (see 16).

But now we are told three times about Jesus' supernatural birth.

1. – Matthew says it (18)

Talking about the birth of *Jesus the Messiah* (18a), Matthew tells us that before Joseph and Mary have slept together, *she was found to be pregnant through the Holy Spirit* (18b).

This is not an argument: it's a statement.

But Joseph has other suspicions.

2. – An angel says it (19-21)

Joseph is clearly a good man: because he assumes Mary has been unfaithful, he needs to divorce her, but doesn't want *to expose her to public disgrace* (19b).

But before he can take this step *an angel of the Lord appeared to him in a dream* (20a). And the angel tells Joseph what Matthew has just told us: that *what is conceived in her is from the Holy Spirit* (20b).

But that's not all.

The angel goes on to tell Joseph that the son Mary gives birth to is to be given *the name Jesus, because he will save his people from their sins* (22b).

The name Jesus was very common in first-century Palestine: it means *Yahweh is salvation* or *Save, Yahweh!* But what is extraordinary here is not the idea of salvation, but the idea of salvation *from sin*.

So *Jesus the Messiah* (18a) is clearly not going to be a political figure: instead he is going to do something that provides forgiveness of sins.

And, as we have already seen, the angel tells Joseph in no uncertain terms that baby Jesus' father is none other than God himself.

3. – Scripture says it (22-23)

Matthew gives us a third reason we can be sure that this is going to be a supernatural birth: he says that this was *to fulfil what the Lord had said through the prophet* (22).

And now he quotes from the Old Testament book of Isaiah, which tells us that *the virgin will conceive and give birth to a son, and they will call him Immanuel* (23, quoting Isa 7:14).

This promise was fulfilled in the 8th century BC (see the larger commentaries for details), but the promises of a child-deliverer in Isaiah chapters 6-12 make something very clear: Isaiah 7:14 is a promise awaiting further fulfilment (see, for example, Isaiah 9:6-7 and 11:1ff).

Mary is the virgin and Immanuel is the name her son will be given. In fact, of course, he was called Jesus (in obedience to the angel, see 21). But the name Immanuel makes it very clear that the salvation which comes about through this child will be a salvation from God: he is *God with us* (23b).

So we have been told three times that Jesus' conception was supernatural. And of course, if God is all-powerful it was no problem for him to cause Mary to become pregnant while still a virgin. This is the Holy Spirit at work (see 18b, 20b), preparing the way so that the God-Man Jesus could restore the relationship between God and human beings.

Joseph certainly seems to get it. He obeys God's message through the angel and takes *Mary home as his wife* (24b).

But, says Matthew, *he did not consummate their marriage until she gave birth to a son* (25a). There is to be no mistake: the birth of this child is supernatural.

And Joseph *gave him the name Jesus* (25b).

C. Jesus: worshipped by Gentiles (2:1-12)

There are lots of things we don't know about the Magi. We don't know how many there were, or exactly where they started their journey.

But we do know that they are *from the east* (1b), and so are Gentiles. And we know that Matthew stresses the theme of *worship* (see 2, 8, 11).

Matthew tells us three things about the Magi.

1. – They follow a star (1-2)

Jesus has been born in Bethlehem, but the Magi arrive in Jerusalem (see 1). They are clear about what they have done and about what they want: *Where is the one who has been born king of the Jews? We saw his star when it rose and have come to worship him* (2).

Through seeing an unusual star they have come to the conclusion that a king has been born. And now they have followed the star.

This is extraordinary. Somehow God has used the superstition of these men to bring them to Jesus, because he is so determined that this baby should be worshipped by Gentiles.

2. – They learn from Scripture (3-8)

King Herod (who is half Jewish) is perturbed by the visit of the Magi, but doesn't know his Bible well enough to be able to get the answer to their question.

So he calls the experts and asks them *where the Messiah was to be born* (4b).

The religious leaders know that the answer is *Bethlehem in Judea* (5a) because they have read the prophecy of Micah in the Scriptures: they are sure that the *ruler who will shepherd my people Israel* is the promised Messiah (see Micah 5:2, 4).

So Herod sends the Magi to Bethlehem and asks them to let him know the baby's exact location, *so that I too may go and worship him* (8b).

Whether they are aware of it or not, the Magi are learning from the Jewish Scriptures. Their superstition has only got them so far: but now they know where they should be going.

3. – They worship Jesus (9-12)

The Magi are still following the star: Matthew tells us that when it stops moving, thus showing that they had reached their destination, *they were overjoyed* (10).

When they see Jesus, *they bowed down and worshipped him* (11a), and give him *gifts of gold, frankincense and myrrh* (11b).

Although Matthew doesn't mention this, he must have known about passages in the Old Testament Scriptures which, in retrospect, point to this event: *May the kings of Tarshish and of distant shores bring tribute to him. May the kings of Sheba and Seba present him with gifts. (…) May gold from Sheba be given to him. (…) Then all nations will be blessed through him* (Psalm 72:10, 15a, 17b; see also Isaiah 60:1-6 and Numbers 24:17a).

We don't know what the Magi meant by what they gave to Jesus as part of their worship. But these gifts are certainly suggestive.

Gold means they see Jesus as a king (which we already know, see 2); incense is something a priest would use when bringing a sacrifice in the temple (see Luke 1:8-10); and myrrh was to be brought later to Jesus' tomb so that his body could be anointed (see John 19:39).

But what we do know is that when Matthew, in this most Jewish of Gospels, gives us the first example of people coming to Jesus, he tells us about Gentiles.

This should make us catch our breath: Gentiles are honouring the Jewish Messiah. And this is much more than a show of respect for a political ruler: the Magi are *worshipping* Jesus.

The picture is gripping: Jesus, the Jewish Messiah, is worshipped by Gentiles. It's like Matthew is turning to us and asking *Are you going to worship him too?*

The Magi decide not to tell Herod how to find Jesus, because they have been *warned in a dream* (12a).

Which leads us to the fourth part of Matthew's Introduction.

D. Jesus: protected by God (2:13-23)

King Herod, and later his son Archelaus, are a danger to Jesus (see 13b and 22a). So Joseph experiences three more dreams sent from God (he has already had one significant dream, see chapter 1:20).

The fact that all the action in these verses is initiated by dreams shows that the main actor here is God. This is underlined by Matthew stressing that these things are fulfilling Old Testament Scripture (see 15, 17-18, 23b).

So this is God protecting his Son.

1. – The first dream (13-18)

Through an angel, God tells Joseph to take his family and *escape to Egypt* (13). The reason is that *Herod is going to search for the child to kill him* (13b).

Of course God is also protecting Joseph and Mary, but it is noteworthy that the focus is on Jesus.

Matthew tells us that this escape to Egypt happens for another reason, too: when the Joseph family come back to Israel, this will be a fulfilment of Hosea's prophecy *Out of Egypt I called my son* (15b, see also Hosea 11:1).

Of course when Hosea wrote about God's son he was talking about the nation of Israel and the escape from slavery in Egypt. But in quoting this verse Matthew is saying something important: what *was* said about Israel (God's son) can *now* be said about Jesus (God's Son).

This is a theme Matthew will return to in his Gospel: Jesus is the fulfilment of the nation of Israel.

Realising the Magi have deliberately failed to tell him where to find the so-called king of the Jews, *Herod gave orders to kill all the boys in Bethlehem and its vicinity who were two years old and under* (16).

Matthew is not excusing Herod's action when he writes that through this butchery *what was said through the prophet Jeremiah was fulfilled* (17, see Jer 31:15).

In the Jeremiah passage Rachel, the ancestress of God's people, is in her tomb weeping because her children are carried away to exile in Babylon. But God responds to this tragedy by stating that *they will return* and that *there is hope* (Jer 31:16b-17a).

Is this what Matthew has in mind here? Just as the tragedy of the exile was followed by the people's return from Babylon, so Herod's killing of the boys in Bethlehem is followed by Jesus' return from Egypt.

Bereavement gives way to hope.

And what is very clear is that, with the first of Joseph's dreams, God is protecting his Son.

2. – The second dream (19-22a)

Matthew tells us that *an angel of the Lord appeared in a dream to Joseph in Egypt* (19), telling him that it was now safe to return to Israel. And this dream comes *after Herod died* (19a): God is still protecting his Son.

So Joseph obeys. But he is afraid because Herod's son Archelaus *was reigning in Judea* (22a).

So more divine protection is needed…

3. – The third dream (22b-23)

We can make an intelligent guess about the content of this dream because it prompts Joseph to move *to the district of Galilee* (22b). He chooses to return to Nazareth, where he and Mary had lived before the birth of Jesus (23a; see also Luke 1:26 and 2:4).

So was fulfilled, says Matthew, *what was said through the prophets, that he would be called a Nazarene* (23b).

Rather than being a direct quotation from the Old Testament, this is a summary of the prophets' expectations of the Messiah. Nazareth doesn't even get a mention in the Old Testament.

But that is precisely the point.

The Messiah, said the prophets, would be a nobody, a backwoodsman. He would grow up *like a root out of dry ground* and would be *despised and rejected by mankind* (Isaiah 53:2a, 3a). As Nathanael said when first told about Jesus: *Nazareth! Can anything good come from there?* (John 1:46a)

By means of these three dreams to Joseph, God has gone to great lengths to protect his Son Jesus.

Matthew has reached the end of his Introduction. He has not just introduced his Gospel, he has also introduced Jesus. And Jesus is the climax of history, with a supernatural birth, worshipped by Gentiles and protected by God.

This is a good opportunity for us to worship Jesus too.

Learning the Gospel

First, learn the four headings in bold; then go back and learn the sub-headings. As you do, many of the details of Matthew's Introduction will come back to you.

This is not difficult, but it is so worthwhile.

Matthew's Introduction

A. Jesus: the climax of history
  1. He's the son of Abraham
  2. He's the son of David
  3. He's the Jewish Messiah

B. Jesus: a supernatural birth
  1. Matthew says it
  2. The angel says it
  3. Scripture says it

C. Jesus: worshipped by Gentiles
  1. They follow a star
  2. They learn from Scripture
  3. They worship Jesus

> **D. Jesus: protected by God**
>   1. The first dream
>   2. The second dream
>   3. The third dream

Meeting the Lord

As you run through Matthew's Introduction in your mind you will find that you will remember some of the details of each paragraph. So as you do, please take time to worship Jesus for all that he is.

Matthew wrote his Gospel not only so that we will *know about* Jesus. He wants us to *meet* him too.

The Matthew experiment is an invitation to do just this.

How to help your memory

1. **Make learning visual** by remembering where the events are on the page of your Bible.
2. **Make learning audible** by learning out loud.
3. **Make learning practical** by doing a little every day.
4. **Make learning enjoyable** by using the experiment to help you pray and worship.

Section One: The Teacher
Matthew 3:1 – 7:29

In his Introduction Matthew has made it very clear that his Gospel is about Jesus. But the last thing we learnt is about the arrival of Jesus and his family in Nazareth when he was still a small boy. Now it is thirty years later: in Section One, Matthew introduces us to Jesus as an adult and to the message he came to proclaim. He is the teacher.

As soon as Jesus was baptised, he went up out of the water.
At that moment heaven was opened,
and he saw the Spirit of God descending like a dove
and alighting on him.
And a voice from heaven said 'This is my Son, whom I love;
with him I am well pleased.'

Matthew 3:16-17

Enjoying the View

Narrative (3:1 – 4:25)

A. His forerunner (3:1-12)
1. John's message (1-6)
2. John's warning (7-10)
3. John's master (11-12)

B. His baptism (3:13-17)
1. John's objection (14)
2. Jesus' explanation (15)
3. God's proclamation (16-17)

C. His temptation (4:1-11)
1. 'Turn these stones into bread' (3-4)
2. 'Throw yourself down from the temple' (5-7)
3. 'Worship me, and I'll give you the world' (8-10)

D. His message (4:12-17)
1. When Jesus preaches it (12)
2. Where Jesus preaches it (13)
3. Why Jesus preaches it (14-16)

E. His team (4:18-22)
1. Jesus: his initiative (18-19, 21)
2. Jesus: his promise (19b)
3. Jesus: his attractiveness (20, 22)

F. His agenda (4:23-25)
1. Proclaiming the kingdom (23a)
2. Many miracles (23b-24)
3. Large crowds (25)

Teaching (5:1 – 7:29)

A. Our character (5:3-12)
    1. Our relationship to God (3-6)
    2. Our relationship to others (7-12)
    3. The rewards Jesus promises (3-12)

B. Our task (5:13-16)
    1. The salt of the earth (13)
    2. The light of the world (14-16)

C. Our righteousness (5:17-48)
    1. Murder (21-26)
    2. Adultery (27-30)
    3. Divorce (31-32)
    4. Oaths (33-37)
    5. Retaliation (38-42)
    6. Hatred (43-47)

D. Our devotion (6:1-18)
    1. Giving (2-4)
    2. Praying (5-15)
    3. Fasting (16-18)

E. Our ambitions (6:19-34)
    1. Wanting stuff (19-24)
    2. Worrying about stuff (25-34)

F. Our relationships (7:1-12)
    1. Don't judge others (1-5)
    2. Don't batter hard hearts (6)
    3. Ask God for help (7-11)

G. Our Jesus-centredness (7:13-27)
    1. The gate and the road (13-14)
    2. The tree and its fruit (15-23)
    3. The wise and foolish builders (24-27)

'When Jesus had finished…' (7:28-29)

Matthew has organised this section – like all the others – so that there is a narrative part followed by a teaching part. The teaching part is what we know as the Sermon on the Mount: Jesus explains what those who decide to follow him will increasingly look like.

But first Matthew has six key things to tell us about Jesus. This is important, because the centre of Jesus' message is Jesus himself. These things form the narrative part of Section One.

Before reading any further, it would be good to read chapter 3:1 – 7:29 of Matthew's Gospel. As you do this, be ready to talk to the Jesus you are reading about and hearing from.

Unpacking the Content

Narrative (3:1 – 4:25)

Everything here is focused on Jesus.

A. His forerunner (3:1-12)

1. – John's message (1-6)

Matthew tells us that *John the Baptist came* (1), announcing the arrival of the kingdom of God: *Repent, for the kingdom of heaven has come near* (2). This is an urgent appeal: since God is about to intervene in human affairs, everyone has to decide if they will turn from their sins and return to God.

Before telling us about the response to this message, Matthew makes it clear that John is a prophet from God: the description of his clothes (see 4) is meant to remind us of Elijah *who wore a garment of hair and a leather belt round his waist* (2 Kings 1:8). Indeed, Zechariah 13:4 tells us that a hair garment was more or less the prophetic uniform. So John, like the Old Testament prophets, is preparing the way for the Messiah.

But the Messiah is much more than a human being. Matthew wants us to know that John *was spoken of through the prophet Isaiah* (3a), who talked of someone proclaiming *Prepare the way for the Lord* (3b, and see Isa 40:3).

This should make us catch our breath: the one who is coming is none other than God himself.

And the response to the message is huge (see 5). Matthew tells us what happened when people streamed out to hear John: *Confessing their sins, they were baptised by him in the River Jordan* (6).

Section One: The Teacher (Matthew 3:1 – 7:29)

2. – John's warning (7-10)

The Pharisees and the Sadducees were two of the most influential groups in first-century Judaism. Matthew tells us that they are coming *to where he was baptising* (7a), presumably to watch and listen rather than to be baptised themselves.

Hence John's warning. He accuses them of relying on their membership of Israel (see 9); instead they must *produce fruit in keeping with repentance* (8). This is urgent because, when God judges, *every tree that does not produce good fruit will be cut down and thrown into the fire* (10b).

3. – John's master (11-12)

The theme of judgment is still present when John talks about the one he is preparing the way for. But first John explains that he is not even worthy to do things a servant does for his master (for example, carry his sandals, see 11).

The coming one will *baptise you with the Holy Spirit* (11b). This is extraordinary because in the Old Testament only God can pour out his Holy Spirit on people. John is saying, too, that the one he is preparing the way for will usher in the new covenant.

All first-century Jews knew that Scripture promised a new covenant, a new relationship with God (see Jer 31:31-34). This would mean that people were forgiven (see Ezek 36:25-27) and had the Holy Spirit living inside them (see Joel 2:28-32).

John is saying that the time is here: the coming one will bring in the new covenant as he pours out the Holy Spirit.

But he will bring judgment too: *His winnowing fork is in his hand, and he will clear his threshing-floor, gathering his wheat into the barn and burning up the chaff with unquenchable fire* (12).

John has not told us the name of the one he is preparing the way for. But now Matthew tells us: *Then Jesus came...* (13a). The conclusion is unmistakeable.

B. His baptism (3:13-17)

1. – John's objection (14)

John has a big problem with the idea of baptising Jesus: *I need to be baptised by you, and do you come to me?* Presumably this is because his baptism is a baptism of repentance; somehow he recognises that Jesus has no sins to repent of. So John tries *to deter him*.

2. – Jesus' explanation (15)

Now Jesus explains to John that *it is proper for us to do this to fulfil all righteousness*. The phrase *to fulfil all righteousness* seems to mean something like *to fulfil God's purpose*.

Although Jesus has no sins of his own, it is God's will that he submits to John's baptism, because in this way he will be identifying with sinners. There is a hint here of what will happen later in the Gospel.

3. – God's proclamation (16-17)

Two things happen as soon as Jesus is baptised.

First, Jesus sees *the Spirit of God descending like a dove and alighting on him* (16b). He is being commissioned for the work he has come to do: it's like God is saying to his Son *Let's save the world!*

And second, the Father speaks from heaven, announcing that *This is my Son, whom I love; with him I am well pleased* (17). The message is clear: Jesus is the Father's pride and joy.

As God the Father proclaims his love for Jesus at his baptism, we see all three Persons of the Trinity: the Son in verse 16a, the Spirit in verse 16b, and the Father in verse 17. The message is clear: God himself is intervening dramatically in human affairs.

The stage is set for what is to come.

C. His temptation (4:1-11)

This account is not here to teach us how to deal with temptation in our own lives. Instead it shows us Jesus being tested as he begins his work.

And it is impossible to read this without thinking of Israel's experience after being rescued from slavery in Egypt. Matthew begins by telling us that Jesus *was led by the Spirit into the wilderness* (1) and that he fasted *for forty days and forty nights* (2): Israel was in the wilderness for forty years.

But what makes this link crystal-clear is that in his encounter with the devil Jesus three times quotes from Deuteronomy chapters 6-8, which are an account of Israel's experience in the wilderness.

And, as we shall see, when Jesus is tested in the wilderness he succeeds where Israel failed.

Matthew tells us the three tests the devil throws at Jesus.

1. – 'Turn these stones into bread' (3-4)

Of course Jesus *was hungry* (2b): this is an obvious temptation for the devil to use to begin his assault.

But there is more here. First-century Jews believed that when the Messiah came he would repeat the manna miracle from the story of Moses and Israel in the wilderness: the reaction to Jesus feeding the 5,000 confirms this (see John 6:14-15).

So this is a temptation to Jesus not only to satisfy his hunger, but also to prove his identity.

But Jesus replies that human beings *shall not live on bread alone, but on every word that comes from the mouth of God* (4). He is quoting from Deuteronomy 8:3, which makes the link with the manna miracle.

2. – 'Throw yourself down from the temple' (5-7)

First-century Jews believed that the Messiah would one day stand on the roof of the temple and proclaim the kingdom of God.

But the devil takes this a step further. He explains that Jesus can throw himself off the temple because God *will command his angels concerning you, and they will lift you up in their hands* (6, quoting Psalm 91:11-12).

Satan is using the Scriptures to entice Jesus to prove his identity again.

For his answer Jesus goes back to the key chapters in Deuteronomy. This time he quotes verse 16 of chapter 6: *Do not put the Lord your God to the test* (7).

3. – 'Worship me, and I'll give you the world' (8-10)

Now the devil shows Jesus *all the kingdoms of the world and their splendour* (8b): he is offering him worldwide dominion.

But at a price. Jesus can have all this, says Satan, *if you will bow down and worship me* (9).

Jesus' mission *was* to be acknowledged by humankind (see Daniel 7:14 and Mt 28:18), but Satan's way for him to achieve this would by-pass the cross. So Jesus again uses the book of Deuteronomy: *Worship the Lord your God, and serve him only* (10b, quoting Deut 6:13).

Jesus will not be moved. He will stay faithful to his Father, and reject the devil: *Away from me, Satan!* (10a)

And now Jesus experiences the truth of Psalm 91, which the devil had quoted from earlier. Matthew tells us that *angels came and attended him* (11).

At last Jesus is ready to proclaim his message.

D. His message (4:12-17)

At the end of this paragraph Matthew will tell us the content of Jesus' message. But first he gives us three important pieces of information.

1. – When Jesus preaches it (12)

The preaching of the message begins *when Jesus heard that John had been put in prison* (12). It was part of Jewish expectation that the coming of the kingdom of God would be heralded by suffering.

So for Jesus, the imprisonment of John the Baptist is like the starting-gun for the beginning of his work of teaching and healing.

2. – Where Jesus preaches it (13)

Jesus moves from Nazareth to Capernaum, *which was by the lake in the area of Zebulun and Naphtali* (13). This is significant because this was a region with a decidedly mixed population: Jews and Gentiles lived alongside each other.

This is a deliberate decision on Jesus' part. He wants Gentiles to hear his message as well as Jews (compare chapter 2:1-12).

3. – Why Jesus preaches it (14-16)

Jesus, says Matthew, moved to Capernaum *to fulfil what was said through the prophet Isaiah* (14). The quotation includes Zebulun and Naphtali and refers to the area as *Galilee of the Gentiles* (15, quoting Isa 9:1-2).

So Jesus obviously has these words from Isaiah in mind as he starts to preach his message: *The people living in darkness have seen a great light; on those living in the land of the shadow of death a light has dawned* (16).

In their original context these Isaiah words were a promise of new hope for Galilee after the devastation of the Assyrian invasion. But now we see a further fulfilment: Jesus has come to bring light into the darkness (see also Isa 9:6-7).

He is preaching as a deliberate fulfilment of Isaiah chapter 9.

And now, for the first time, we hear Jesus preaching his message: *Repent, for the kingdom of heaven has come near* (17). This is exactly the same message John the Baptist had preached as he prepared the way for Jesus (see chapter 3:1): as soon as John is no longer able to preach it (see 12), Jesus the Teacher starts proclaiming the message himself.

The kingdom of God is not a geographical kingdom; it is present wherever God is reigning in human hearts. And in the teaching part of Section One we will see that being in the kingdom changes people radically (see chapters 5, 6 and 7).

This is also part of the message of Jesus the Teacher.

E. His team (4:18-22)

As Matthew shows us Jesus beginning to collect his disciple team, we see three things about Jesus.

1. – Jesus: his initiative (18-19, 21)

The two pairs of brothers (Simon and Andrew, James and John) are not volunteers: Jesus is calling them. The initiative is all his: *Come, follow me* (19a, see also 21b). They have already known him for a number of months, but today is to be the day of decision.

2. – Jesus: his promise (19b)

Jesus' call also contains a promise. If these men decide to follow him, *I will send you out to fish for people* (19b). The message Jesus has come to bring is one they will take to others, and others will decide to join the Jesus team too.

3. – Jesus: his attractiveness (20, 22)

This is a huge step for these four men. It doesn't just involve *following*; it also involves *leaving*. Simon and Andrew leave *their nets* (20); James and John leave *the boat and their father* (22).

The message is clear. Jesus is such an attractive figure that it is worth leaving everything, including family, possessions and occupation, to follow him.

It may well be that Matthew is encouraging us, his readers, to follow the example of Simon, Andrew, James and John.

F. His agenda (4:23-25)

This is like a summary paragraph at the end of Section One's narrative part. It sums up Jesus' priorities going forward.

1. – Proclaiming the kingdom (23a)

This will come as no surprise to us: John the Baptist preached it (see chapter 3:1), and Jesus has started preaching it too (see chapter 4:17). He does this as he travels around Galilee, *teaching in their synagogues* (23a).

Presumably the disciples are accompanying him. But the focus is on Jesus.

2. – Many miracles (23b-24)

Matthew underlines how extraordinary this is. Jesus is *healing every disease and illness among the people* (23b). Now we get a list of what that might have involved: *those suffering severe pain, the demon-possessed, those having seizures, and the paralysed* (24).

And, says Matthew, *he healed them* (24b).

Jesus is showing his desire to change the lives of suffering people. But the miracles do more than this: they point to the reality and vitality of the kingdom Jesus is proclaiming.

3. – Large crowds (25)

Jesus is big news! There is huge interest in this man: *Large crowds from Galilee, the Decapolis, Jerusalem, Judea and the region across the Jordan followed him* (25).

This is part of Jesus' agenda too: he is deliberately attracting the crowds.

We don't know how many of these people were only interested in the miracles and not in the message. But we do know that Jesus is calling all of us to follow him and enter the kingdom of God.

Teaching (5:1 – 7:29)

The teaching part of Section One is known as the Sermon on the Mount, because Jesus *went up on a mountainside and sat down* (1).

Matthew tells us that *his disciples came to him, and he began to teach them* (1b-2a). This doesn't mean that Jesus is avoiding the crowds – after all, he has spent time doing things that have attracted many people (see chapter 4:24-25). So it's not just the disciples who hear Jesus teaching: the crowds are listening too (see chapter 7:28-29).

The message of his teaching answers an important question: When people make the decision to follow Jesus and come into the kingdom of God, what will they look like? How does being a Jesus disciple change someone?

Jesus answers that question by pointing to seven aspects of disciples' lives. The first is *our character*.

A. Our character (5:3-12)

This paragraph contains eight sayings which all begin with the word *blessed* and are known as *beatitudes* (from the Latin word for *blessing*). The people with these characteristics, says Jesus, are blessed.

The problem is that we don't really use that word in modern English. *Happy* is no better, because that just describes a psychological state. A better translation might be *fortunate* or *enviable*. In other words: if you have this characteristic, it's because God is at work in your life.

1. – Our relationship to God (3-6)

If we are *poor in spirit* (3) we recognise our poverty before God: we are, spiritually speaking, bankrupt. People with this quality know that there is nothing in them which could recommend them to God.

Those who mourn (4) are sad because of their spiritual poverty: they are aware that they are not as they should be. This is about recognising that we are sinners before a holy God.

The meek are to be envied (5) because they don't big themselves up: they know that they are spiritual pygmies.

And *those who hunger and thirst for righteousness* (6) are not satisfied with things as they are: they long to become more and more the people God made them to be.

2. – Our relationship to others (7-12)

Jesus' disciples are *merciful* (7): they are not judgmental. We can all think of situations where we have seen a mistake someone has made, and we have written them off. Being merciful means realising that there may be all kinds of reasons why that person is behaving that way.

People who decide to follow Jesus become more and more *pure in heart* (8). They will not have mixed motives as they relate to others: instead their interaction with others will be genuine.

Then, says Jesus, *blessed are the peacemakers* (9). This is about people who, rather than just looking the other way when confronted by broken relationships, try to do something. They want to help both sides tear down the wall and build a bridge instead.

We know that the next beatitude is the last, because the reward promised is the same as in the first beatitude (compare 10b with 3b). Now Jesus tells us that those who follow him will be *persecuted because of righteousness* (10). This is different from all that Jesus has said so far: this is not about how *we* relate to *others*, but about how *others* relate to *us*.

This is so important that there is an add-on to explain it more fully: *Blessed are you when people insult you, persecute you and falsely say all kinds of evil against you* (11). But this time, instead of saying *because of righteousness,* he says *because of me* (11b).

And immediately Jesus talks of the reward awaiting such people: *Rejoice and be glad, because great is your reward in heaven, for in the same way they persecuted the prophets who were before you* (12). The early church took this encouragement to heart (see Acts 5:40-41).

3. – The rewards Jesus promises (3-12)

Jesus stresses here that no one ever loses out by becoming his disciple. For every characteristic in this list there is a reward to be expected, because God loves to give gifts to his children.

The rewards involve knowing we are accepted by God (see 3b, 10b), the assurance that we are forgiven (see 4b), the certainty that we will live one day in the perfect, renewed creation (see 5b), and being satisfied as we realise we are being changed in preparation for this (see 6b).

But there are more rewards still! Jesus promises us that he will show us mercy (see 7b), that we will experience him perfectly in the new world (see 8b), and that we will be recognised as his children (see 9b).

To sum up all these rewards, Jesus' disciples are *blessed*; they are to be envied because God is at work in their lives. But let's be clear. They have not earned this blessing by being extraordinary people: they come to Jesus recognising their need.

And he starts to change them and reward them.

B. Our task (5:13-16)

Anyone who reads the beatitudes carefully will know that such people will change the world. But now Jesus makes clear that this task he gives his disciples is one they are to accomplish not as individuals but *together*.

To spell this out he uses two images to describe the task of the Jesus community.

1. – The salt of the earth (13)

In the first century salt was used as an antiseptic and as a preservative. So in calling his disciples *the salt of the earth* (13a), Jesus is saying that they are to be both different and involved.

Salt is *different* and must stay different: *If the salt loses its saltiness, how can it be made salty again?* (13b) So the Jesus community must be different from the world around: this will involve different moral standards.

But salt is also *involved*: it must soak into the meat. In the same way, disciples are not to be socially segregated but to penetrate society.

Our task, says Jesus, is to be a good influence on the world we are part of.

2. – The light of the world (14-16)

Jesus makes it clear: *A town built on a hill cannot be hidden* (14). People don't hide a lamp; instead they put it on its stand, and it gives light to everyone in the house (15).

This second image repeats the lessons of the first. The Jesus community is to be spiritually and morally distinct. But at the same time we are to affect the surrounding culture: the world is to be *different* because of the influence of those who follow Jesus.

The salt must soak into the meat and the light must shine into the darkness: if a house at night is dark, don't blame the house!

One way in which this influence will occur is simply through our example. Jesus tells us to *let your light shine before others, that they may see your good deeds and glorify your Father in heaven* (16). As Jesus disciples live more and more in the way the Sermon on the Mount describes, there will be people who conclude that this must be a supernatural community and turn to God.

If the followers of Jesus are the light of the world, it is only because *he* is the light of the world (see John 8:12, fulfilling Isa 49:6).

But our task is clear.

C. Our righteousness (5:17-48)

Jesus says that he has not come *to abolish the Law or the Prophets* (17): he is talking about the whole of what we would call the Old Testament. Instead he is going *to fulfil them* (17b).

That word *fulfil* is key. Jesus is bringing everything that the Old Testament looked forward to: he is the culmination of the revelation because he fulfils every aspect of it.

So there is a warning here for people who want to lop off parts of Scripture: they will *be called least in the kingdom of heaven* (19). But this doesn't mean that Jesus is looking for slavish obedience to rules and regulations: *I tell you that unless your righteousness surpasses that of the Pharisees and the teachers of the law, you will certainly not enter the kingdom of heaven* (20).

The Pharisees were known for their righteousness, but it was all on the cover. What Jesus wants to see in his disciples is a relationship of love and obedience to God which is more than a literal observance of regulations.

He is looking for righteousness *in the heart* (see chapter 5:8).

But now a question arises: what does this look like in practice? We find the answer in the six examples Jesus gives us. Each time he begins by saying something like *You have heard that it was said*, which introduces a quotation from the Law (or sometimes a corruption of it); this is followed by the words *But I tell you*: now Jesus explains how the principle of heart-righteousness transcends the common understanding of the Law.

This will become clearer as we look at the examples.

1. – Murder (21-26)

You have heard that it was said leads to Jesus quoting the sixth commandment: *You shall not murder* (21, see Exod 20:13).

But I tell you: now Jesus goes deeper. *Anyone who is angry with a brother or sister will be subject to judgment* (22a). Even saying to someone *You fool!* puts us *in danger of the fire of hell* (22b).

Jesus is focusing on the attitude in the heart. In order to show us what obeying this command looks like in practice, Jesus paints two pictures for us (see verses 23-24 and 25-26).

If I have come to worship God and am aware of a broken relationship, I must *first go and be reconciled* (24). And if someone is taking me to court I should *settle matters quickly* (25).

So the purpose of the *Do not murder* command is that, instead of harbouring anger against someone or despising them, we should work for reconciliation and peace.

2. – Adultery (27-30)

You have heard that it was said introduces the seventh commandment: *You shall not commit adultery* (27, see Exod 20:14).

But I tell you: Jesus is not just interested in actions. *Anyone who looks at a woman lustfully has already committed adultery with her in his heart* (28). To be tempted, of course, is not a sin; but if we feed that temptation and make a sex film in our minds, we have crossed the line and have become adulterers.

This is a much deeper righteousness than the righteousness of the religious leaders.

Now Jesus talks about our eye or our hand causing us to fall into sin (see 29-30). The eye may refer to something we look at, and the hand to something we do. The eye must be gouged out and the hand cut off. Of course Jesus doesn't mean this literally: he means that we need to take action.

That's important because it's serious. Jesus tells us twice that *it is better for you to lose one part of your body than for your whole body to be thrown into hell* (29b, 30b).

3. – Divorce (31-32)

It has been said, says Jesus, and quotes from the Old Testament Law again: *Anyone who divorces his wife must give her a certificate of divorce* (31, see Deut 24:1-4).

But the quotation is not exact. In Deuteronomy it is about a man who has divorced his wife; after she has been married to someone else, he is not permitted to marry her again.

But what Jesus is saying here is that divorce is not something to be taken lightly: no one should divorce *except for sexual immorality* (32).

This is about righteousness in action.

4. – Oaths (33-37)

You have heard that it was said leads into *Do not break your oath...* (33). Old Testament Law prohibited dishonest and unfulfilled oaths (eg Lev 19:12), but otherwise allowed them.

But Jesus goes deeper: *But I tell you, do not swear an oath at all* (34a). If the Pharisees took an oath they did it *by heaven* or *by the earth,* or *by Jerusalem* (34-35): this meant that if they didn't keep their oath they weren't guilty because they had not sworn *by God*.

But Jesus, looking for a greater righteousness, wants plain, honest speech without the need for oaths. He tells his disciples that *all you need to say is simply Yes or No; anything beyond this comes from the evil one* (37).

Truthfulness should be at the heart (and *in* the heart) of every Jesus follower.

5. – Retaliation (38-42)

Once again, Jesus begins with *You have heard that it was said*. Now he is talking about retaliation: *Eye for eye, and tooth for tooth* (38, see Exod 21:24). It looks like the religious leaders of first-century Israel were taking this law out of the law courts and into the realm of personal relationships. They were justifying revenge.

But I tell you, says Jesus, *do not resist an evil person* (39a). This is not just rejecting retaliation; it is rejecting resistance too: *If anyone slaps you on the right cheek, turn to them the other cheek also* (39b). This is describing a blow with the back of the hand, a sign of utter contempt.

So if someone wants my shirt, I should throw in my coat too; if a Roman soldier forces me to carry his pack for a mile, I should volunteer for another mile; and if someone wants to borrow something from me I should not turn them away (see 40-42).

This is strong stuff. It is all part of the greater righteousness which Jesus wants to see in his disciples.

6. – Hatred (43-47)

You have heard that it was said, says Jesus: *Love your neighbour and hate your enemy* (43). Jesus is affirming that the Old Testament Law commands love to one's neighbour (see Lev 19:18); but there is no command to hate one's enemy.

This is a step further than the previous example Jesus gave us. Now we are not just being commanded to not resist an enemy, but to actively love them. And loving them will make me want to pray for them too (see 44).

If we behave like this, says Jesus, we will be showing that we are *children of your Father in heaven* (45a). This, after all, is the way God behaves, who *causes his sun to rise on the evil and the good* (45).

And Jesus underlines this by saying that if we only love those who love us, we are no better than people who don't acknowledge God at all: *Do not even pagans do that?* (47b)

This command to unconditional love ends Jesus' list of six examples of the deeper righteousness which he is looking for in those who follow him. He is not asking for the superficial obedience to God's law which characterised the religious leaders of first-century Judaism. He wants to see heart-righteousness.

Jesus sums it up for his disciples and would-be disciples. They should long to *be perfect, therefore, as your heavenly Father is perfect* (48). We are not to be people who just keep rules; we are to live our lives for God.

D. Our devotion (6:1-18)

Jesus is still talking about righteousness here. Now he tackles three areas that the Pharisees took very seriously, but for the wrong reasons.

The principle is clear: *Be careful not to practise your righteousness in front of others to be seen by them* (1a). Those who do these things in order to impress others, Jesus warns his disciples, *will have no reward from your Father in heaven* (1b).

Now Jesus explains what that means in practice.

1. – Giving (2-4)

When disciples give to those in need, says Jesus, they should *not announce it with trumpets… to be honoured by others* (2). If they do, they are *hypocrites*, and that is all the reward they are going to get (see 2b).

Instead, such giving should be *in secret* (4a), in other words without drawing attention to itself. Jesus promises that *your Father, who sees what is done in secret, will reward you* (4).

Tantalisingly, Jesus doesn't explain what this reward is. Is it a reward now – his blessing on our lives? Or is it a reward later, in the new age? The answer is probably Yes!

2. – Praying (5-15)

Jesus tells his disciples not to pray in public *to be seen by others*: if they do, they are *like the hypocrites* (5). Once again, Jesus says that the admiration of others is the only reward they are going to get.

Instead *Go into your room, close the door and pray to your Father, who is unseen. Then your Father, who sees what is done in secret, will reward you* (6).

Having read what Jesus said about giving, we might expect him to stop at this point. But he has more to say about prayer. He tells us to *not keep on babbling like pagans, for they think they will be heard because of their many words* (7). This is unnecessary because God our Father already knows what we need (see 8).

And now Jesus gives his disciples a pattern prayer (see 9-13). It has five main ingredients.

First, acknowledging God. The prayer begins *Our Father in heaven, hallowed be your name* (9). The emphasis on calling God *Father* is one we have already seen in this teaching part of Section One (see chapter 5:16, 48), and at Jesus' baptism we heard God say about Jesus *This is my Son* (chapter 3:17).

The conclusion is staring us in the face: if we have come to know Jesus we can call *his* Father *our* Father.

As they pray, disciples are in the presence of a holy God they can call Father.

Second, the glory of God. The prayer's first request is *Your kingdom come, your will be done* (10) because the glory of God is more important than anything else. The kingdom coming is about more and more people coming to acknowledge Jesus and joyfully submitting to God's rule in their lives; God's will being done is about his plan for the world being perfectly fulfilled.

Third, personal needs. The request *Give us today our daily bread* (11) is a catch-all: we can ask God to fulfil all our needs (which is not the same as him satisfying all our *wants*).

Fourth, forgiveness of sins. Asking God to *forgive us our debts* (12a) is asking for forgiveness, which is our greatest need as sinners who have got lost. Interestingly, Jesus assumes we will be able to add *as we also have forgiven our debtors* (12b).

If we jump on for a moment we will hear Jesus explaining what he means (see 14-15). If we refuse to forgive others, then any prayer we pray for our own forgiveness is hypocrisy (which Jesus has already condemned, see 2 and 5).

And fifth, spiritual protection. The request *Lead us not into temptation* (13a) might better be understood as asking God to protect us from *testing*: but if he does allow us to be tested we can pray *Deliver us from the evil one* (13b).

Jesus doesn't necessarily mean we should pray this prayer word for word, though there is of course no harm in that. But the ingredients of this prayer should impact all our own praying.

3. – Fasting (6:16-18)

Now Jesus is talking about *the hypocrites* again, who look mournful when they fast (see 16a). The issue, once again, is motive: *they disfigure their faces to show others they are fasting* (16). If the aim of some people in fasting is simply to impress others, that is all the reward they are going to get (see 16b).

And so we know what Jesus will say next. We are to do what we can *so that it will not be obvious to others that you are fasting* (18a). But there is someone who sees, because *your Father, who sees what is done in secret, will reward you* (18b).

Another word for hypocrisy is *play-acting*. Jesus is saying to disciples and would-be disciples that he is looking for *reality* in their devotion to God.

Nothing else will do.

E. Our ambitions (6:19-34)

Jesus shifts his focus now from religious acts to everyday life. But the context is the same: disciples live their lives in relationship with God their Father (see 26, 32).

Knowing and experiencing this will have a huge effect on what we live for. When we start following Jesus our ambitions will change.

This is another part of the *greater righteousness* Jesus is looking for in his disciples (see chapter 5:20).

1. – Wanting stuff (19-24)

Jesus has no problem with us collecting treasure; the question is: where are we keeping it?

The wrong place for our treasure is *on earth, where moths and vermin destroy, and where thieves break in and steal* (19b). Wanting more and more material things is a dead-end street, because we are bound to lose them one way or another.

The right place for our treasure is *in heaven, where moths and vermin do not destroy, and where thieves do not break in and steal* (20b). Jesus explains *where* this treasure is, but not *what* it is: presumably it is about a life joyfully submitted to God our Father.

Jesus sums it up by telling us that *where your treasure is, there your heart will be also* (21). What I think about most tells me what I treasure most: is it material possessions or is it my heavenly Father and his glory?

The eye, says Jesus, *is the lamp of the body* (22a). The eye helps us to see where we're going, so this is about purposeful living: what we do with the possessions we have. Do we keep them for ourselves or are we ready to share?

If your eyes are healthy (22b) is a picture-language way of talking about being generous; *if your eyes are unhealthy* (23a) is a way of talking about being mean. This is clear from the Old Testament proverb which says *He who has a good eye will be blessed, for he gives his bread to the poor* (Prov 22:9, literal translation).

Jesus is saying that being generous with what we have will do us good: *your whole body will be full of light* (22b), while being stingy will have the opposite effect: *your whole body will be full of darkness* (23b). This is enough to make us ask ourselves the question: *What am I living for – possessions or God?*

We have to make a choice, because *no one can serve two masters* (24a). Someone, or something, has to have priority in our lives. So a decision needs to be made, because we *cannot serve both God and Money* (24b).

If *wanting stuff* is one unhealthy preoccupation, Jesus now mentions another.

2. – Worrying about stuff (25-34)

Jesus says here that it is not only pointless to worry about food, drink or clothes: it is wrong, too: *Do not worry* (25a).

He gives us at least three reasons for this. First, *is not life more* than material things? (see 25b); second, we are *much more valuable* than the birds, *and yet your heavenly Father feeds them* (26, and see also 28-30); and third, worrying doesn't actually achieve anything: *Can any of you by worrying add a single hour to your life?* (27)

Jesus makes the point even clearer by adding that *the pagans run after all these things* (32a), whereas as disciples of Jesus we can be sure that *your heavenly Father knows that you need them* (32b).

We know what *not* to do; now Jesus tells us the positive side: *Seek first his kingdom and his righteousness* (33a). Here is the heavenly treasure which should be preoccupying us (see 20). And if we get our priorities right in this way, Jesus promises us that we will experience God looking after our material needs: *...and all these things will be given to you as well* (33b).

Almost as an afterthought Jesus adds something else we should not worry about: *Do not worry about tomorrow, for tomorrow will worry about itself* (34). We can trust God our heavenly Father with our future, too.

Life in a world like ours can be a struggle: *Each day has enough trouble of its own* (34b). So it's important to make sure that we have the right ambitions. I need to say *No* to wanting and worrying about material things and keep saying *Yes* to God, his kingdom and his righteousness.

F. Our relationships (7:1-12)

This part of Jesus' teaching is all about relationships. This includes the emphasis on prayer in verses 7-11: verse 12 shows that Jesus mentions prayer in the context of how we relate to others.

1. – Don't judge others (1-5)

Jesus' saying here is well-known: *Do not judge, or you too will be judged* (1). The word is ambiguous. What is being condemned is self-righteous fault-finding.

Which is what Jesus' description of a funny situation makes clear: *Why do you look at the speck of sawdust in your brother's eye and pay no attention to the plank in your own eye?* (3) Instead of just a larger speck of sawdust, it's a plank! In other words, it's ridiculous to write others off when we are far from perfect ourselves.

But there are some situations in which it is right to make a judgment about others.

2. – Don't batter hard hearts (6)

This seems to be the meaning of what Jesus says here. He tells us to *not give dogs what is sacred* and *not throw your pearls to pigs* (6a).

Jesus doesn't explain what he is getting at. Does he mean that there is no value in telling people the gospel again and again if they are hardened against it? It may even make their hearts harder, because *they may trample them under their feet, and turn and tear you to pieces* (6b).

Of course hard hearts don't have to *stay* hard: the Holy Spirit can cause people to become open to the good news. And we can pray that he will do it.

3. – Ask God for help (7-11)

If disciples are not to be writing others off and not to be bombarding hard-hearted people with their message, they will need to ask God for help. Jesus makes it very clear that such prayers will be answered: *Ask and it will be given to you; seek and you will find; knock and the door will be opened to you* (7).

Jesus underlines this with a short parable in the form of two questions: *Which of you, if your son asks for bread, will give him a stone? Or if he asks for a fish, will give him a snake?* (9-10)

He explains it too. If we give good gifts to our children, *though you are evil* (11a), *how much more will your Father in heaven give good gifts to those who ask him!* (11b)

This is because God wants to help us have healthy relationships with those we know. Jesus sums it up by telling us to *do to others what you would have them do to you, for this sums up the Law and the Prophets* (12).

Such teaching is common in other ethical systems, but there it's nearly always negative (ie *Don't do to others what you wouldn't like others to do to you*). The righteousness that Jesus is looking for in his disciples runs much deeper.

G. Our Jesus-centredness (7:13-29)

Jesus' message in the teaching part of Section One has been about how his disciples should live. As he reaches the climax of his Sermon on the Mount, Jesus uses three pictures which enable him to ask his listeners three questions.

1. – The gate and the road (13-14)

There are two gates, and each gate gets you onto a road. Jesus tells us that *wide is the gate and broad is the road that leads to destruction, and many enter through it* (13b). But there is another possibility: *But small is the gate and narrow the road that leads to life, and only a few find it* (14).

The message is clear: *Enter through the narrow gate* (13a). The question Jesus is asking us is *Have you started the journey?*

2. – The tree and its fruit (15-23)

You can recognise whether a tree is healthy or not by looking at its fruit: *Every good tree bears good fruit, but a bad tree bears bad fruit* (17).

Jesus applies this principle in two ways.

First, it can help us to spot false teachers: *they come to you in sheep's clothing but inwardly they are ferocious wolves* (15). At first sight they may look like genuine members of the Jesus community, but, says Jesus, *by their fruit you will recognise them* (16a, 20). There is a warning of judgment here too: *Every tree that does not bear good fruit is cut down and thrown into the fire* (19).

Second, it can help us to see whether we have really become disciples. It's not just about being able to say *Lord, Lord* to Jesus (21a); the person accepted into the kingdom of God is *the one who does the will of my Father who is in heaven* (21b).

Jesus is not talking about prophesying, driving out demons and performing miracles: these are not a ticket into the kingdom (see 22). If we are not showing the fruit of the deeper righteousness this sermon has been talking about, this is evidence that there has never been a relationship with Jesus, and we will hear solemn words on Judgment Day: *I never knew you. Away from me, you evildoers!* (23)

The question Jesus is asking us is *Are you the real thing?*

3. – The wise and foolish builders (24-27)

The third picture is about two men, each building a house: but the foundations are very different. One *built his house on the rock* (24b), while the other *built his house on sand* (26b). When a storm comes, the first builder's house *did not fall* (25), while the second builder's *fell with a great crash* (27b).

The first builder, says Jesus, is *a wise man* (24) and the second builder is *a foolish man* (26).

Jesus spells out his message: *Everyone who hears these words of mine and puts them into practice is like a wise man* (24); *everyone who hears these words of mine and does not put them into practice is like a foolish man* (26).

Real wisdom is not just *hearing* what Jesus says, but *doing* what Jesus says too. Obeying him is the only firm foundation.

The question Jesus is asking now is *Are you doing what I say?*

All through the teaching part of Section One we have been listening to Jesus. But now he is turning to us and, using these three pictures, asking us the questions: *Have you started the journey? Are you the real thing? And are you doing what I say?*

The answers to those questions will help us to see if we really are in relationship with Jesus.

Now Matthew signals that we have reached the end of Section One: *When Jesus had finished saying these things...* (28a).

But, much more importantly, he tells us that *the crowds were amazed at his teaching* (28b) because he was so different from their teachers of the law: *he taught as one who had authority* (29a).

And if we want to know what that authority looks like, Matthew will invite us to read Section Two of his Gospel.

Learning the Gospel

The structure of Section One makes it easy to learn.

Start with the narrative part. Just learn the headings in bold, and remember that saying them aloud will make this much easier.

Now learn the sub-headings. As you do, you will find yourself remembering all kinds of details in what Matthew writes. If you repeat these a number of times it will not be long before you have the narrative part in your mind.

Now do the same with the teaching part of the section: first learn the headings in bold, and then go back to learn the sub-headings.

You will find this easier to do if you have arranged with a friend to meet up after you have both learnt Section One.

Learning Section One can be done in about ten minutes. And it's worth it.

Section One: The Teacher

Narrative

A. His forerunner
1. John's message
2. John's warning
3. John's master

B. His baptism
1. John's objection
2. Jesus' explanation
3. God's proclamation

C. His temptation
1. 'Turn these stones into bread'
2. 'Throw yourself down from the temple'
3. 'Worship me, and I'll give you the world'

D. His message
1. When Jesus preaches it
2. Where Jesus preaches it
3. Why Jesus preaches it

E. His team
1. Jesus: his initiative
2. Jesus: his promise
3. Jesus: his attractiveness

F. His agenda
1. Proclaiming the kingdom
2. Many miracles
3. Large crowds

Teaching

A. Our character
1. Our relationship to God
2. Our relationship to others
3. The rewards Jesus promises

- **B. Our task**
  1. The salt of the earth
  2. The light of the world
- **C. Our righteousness**
  1. Murder
  2. Adultery
  3. Divorce
  4. Oaths
  5. Retaliation
  6. Hatred
- **D. Our devotion**
  1. Giving
  2. Praying
  3. Fasting
- **E. Our ambitions**
  1. Wanting stuff
  2. Worrying about stuff
- **F. Our relationships**
  1. Don't judge others
  2. Don't batter hard hearts
  3. Ask God for help
- **G. Our Jesus-centredness**
  1. The gate and the road
  2. The tree and its fruit
  3. The wise and foolish builders

'When Jesus had finished…'

Meeting the Lord

Once you have committed the structure to memory, start to tell the events of the section to yourself, or to a friend, including as many details as you remember. As you do this, the Holy Spirit will be using the Jesus story in your life.

This will get you praying and worshipping too.

Section One: The Teacher (Matthew 3:1 – 7:29)

As you run through Section One's narrative part in your mind, take time to thank God for John the Baptist's message and especially for what he says about Jesus; thank *God* for his words at Jesus' baptism; thank *Jesus* for his faithfulness when tempted by Satan.

Now do the same with the teaching part of the section. Talk to Jesus about what he says disciples should look like; ask him to be at work in you by his Spirit in all these areas of life.

This is the Matthew experiment: as you re-tell Matthew you will be meeting the Lord.

Section Two: The Lord
Matthew 8:1 – 11:1

At the end of Section One Matthew has pointed out the crowd's astonishment at the authority with which Jesus teaches. Now, in the narrative part of Section Two, we see the lordship of Jesus in action, while the teaching part has Jesus giving the twelve disciples his authority to proclaim the message of the kingdom of God in preaching and in works of power. All of this pushes one question to the front of our minds: *Who is this man?*

> Then he got up and rebuked the winds and the waves,
> and it was completely calm.
> The men were amazed and asked
> 'What kind of man is this?
> Even the winds and the waves obey him!'
> Matthew 8:26b-27

Section Two: The Lord (Matthew 8:1 – 11:1) 51

Enjoying the View

Narrative (8:1 – 9:38)

A. Who Jesus loves (8:1-17)
1. He heals a leper (1-4)
2. He heals a centurion's servant (5-13)
3. He heals Peter's mother-in-law (14-15)

B. Two warnings for disciples (8:18-22)
1. A man who claims too much (18-20)
2. A man who offers too little (21-22)

C. Where Jesus is Lord (8:23 – 9:8)
1. He rules nature (23-27)
2. He crushes evil (28-34)
3. He forgives sin (9:1-8)

D. Two stories for disciples (9:9-17)
1. Jesus calls Matthew and eats with sinners (9-13)
2. Jesus predicts a radical break with Judaism (14-17)

E. What Jesus does (9:18-34)
1. He gives life (18-26)
2. He opens eyes (27-31)
3. He loosens tongues (32-34)

F. Two facts for disciples (9:35-38)
1. What Jesus feels (35-36)
2. What Jesus wants (37-38)

Teaching (10:1 – 11:1)

A. Mission: its authority (10:1-4)
1. Where it's from (1)
2. Who it's for (2-4)

B. Mission: its description (10:5-15)
1. Proclamation to Jews, not Gentiles (5-6)
2. Proclamation in word and deed (7-8)
3. Proclamation while trusting God (9-15)

C. Mission: its opposition (10:16-25)
1. Arrest and trial (16-20)
2. Betrayal and hatred (21-23)
3. Being treated like Jesus (24-25)

D. Mission: its secret (10:26-42)
1. There is a Judgment Day (26-33)
2. This is part of the plan (34-36)
3. There are two responses (37-42)

'When Jesus had finished…' (11:1)

Once again, Matthew has structured this section with a narrative part followed by a teaching part: this is a real help for the memory.

The narrative part contains three miracle blocks, with three miracles in each (blocks A, C and E): these demonstrate Jesus' authority in every area of life. Each miracle block is followed by a block of two elements which tell us something about what it means to be a Jesus disciple (blocks B, D and F).

In the teaching part of Section Two Jesus the Lord is preparing the disciples as he sends them out to proclaim his message about the arrival of the kingdom. So his theme is mission.

It would be good to read though Matthew 8:1 – 11:1 before reading any further in *The Matthew Experiment*. Be ready to meet Jesus: it is only a short step from reading to worship.

Unpacking the Content

Narrative (8:1 – 9:38)

The focus in this opening part of Section Two is immediately on the authority of Jesus. Matthew uses the word three times (see chapter 8:9 and chapter 9:6-8), but in everything Jesus says and does he demonstrates his authority: he is Jesus the Lord.

The structure of this narrative part is intriguing. By interweaving Jesus' powerful works with his words about what following him involves, Matthew is letting us know that becoming a Jesus disciple is the natural response to seeing his authority: since Jesus is like this, how can we *not* decide to join his team?

We begin with the first block of three miracles.

A. Who Jesus loves (8:1-17)

There is a simple answer to this: he loves outsiders. The incidents we are going to read about are not random stories: Matthew wants us to see that Jesus cares for people who might feel excluded from the life of Israel.

1. – He heals a leper (1-4)

When we read that *a man with leprosy came and knelt before* Jesus (2a), we are probably to see this as referring to any skin disease. This would have been unsightly, and others would avoid contact with this man because of fear of infection.

But the man himself seems confident about Jesus' power: *Lord, if you are willing, you can make me clean* (2b). (*Lord* here may mean much the same as *Sir*.)

Before Jesus says anything, he does something: he *reached out his hand and touched the man* (3a). There is no need for Jesus to do this: it's a sign of deep compassion. This leper might not have been touched by another human being for years: we can only imagine how he feels when Jesus touches him. And as he touches him Jesus says *I am willing.* (…) *Be clean!* (3a)

Matthew tells us that *immediately he was cleansed of his leprosy* (3b). Jesus is more infectious than the disease! This is his authority in action.

2. – He heals a centurion's servant (5-13)

The centurion is a Gentile; we don't know if his servant is a Jew or a Gentile. But Jesus shows that he is willing to help a Gentile representative of the Roman occupying power: he offers to come and heal the man's servant (see 7).

The centurion says that he doesn't deserve this, and explains that he is *a man under authority* (9). This authority means that he is used to giving commands and having them obeyed; and he is sure that Jesus has authority like this: *Just say the word, and my servant will be healed* (8b).

Jesus is astonished because this man is a Gentile: he tells his disciples that *I have not found anyone in Israel with such great faith* (10). And he adds two things which will surprise everyone who is listening.

First, says Jesus, many Gentiles will one day be part of the messianic banquet in the new age: *Many will come from the east and the west and take their places at the feast with Abraham, Isaac and Jacob* (11). That is astonishing enough: but there is more.

Second, many Jewish people will not be welcome in what we often call heaven, for *the subjects of the kingdom will be thrown outside, into the darkness, where there will be weeping and gnashing of teeth* (12).

Does Matthew want us to read the words *Many will come from the east* (11a) and remember that the first people in his Gospel to visit the baby Jesus were *Magi from the east* (chapter 2:1)?

Jesus has more good news for the centurion: *Let it be done just as you believed it would* (13a). And Matthew tells us matter-of-factly that *his servant was healed at that moment* (13b).

The centurion was right about the authority of Jesus (see 8-9).

3. – He heals Peter's mother-in-law (14-15)

Peter's mother-in-law is *lying in bed with a fever* (14b). Jesus doesn't say anything: instead *he touched her hand and the fever left her* (15a).

In first-century Jewish culture women had a secondary position: in some situations they were seen as outsiders. But Jesus – the man with authority – shows this woman the same love he had shown the unclean leper and the Roman centurion.

We have read about three miracles which demonstrate Jesus' authority in action as he heals outsiders. But there is more: after sunset Jesus sets free *many who were demon-possessed* and heals *all who were ill* (16). In other words Matthew has only highlighted three examples among many.

And this is *to fulfil what was spoken through the prophet Isaiah* (17a). This is the sixth time that Matthew uses this fulfilment formula or one like it (see chapter 1:22-23, 2:14-15, 17-18, 23; 4:13-16): he is underlining that Jesus fulfils the Old Testament revelation (see also chapter 5:17).

Matthew quotes Isaiah's words about the Servant of the Lord who was to come: *He took up our infirmities and bore our diseases* (17b, see also Isa 53:4). So Jesus not only infected those he healed with *his* wholeness; he also allowed himself to be infected by *their* disease.

By ending his first block in Section Two's narrative part with a quotation from Isaiah chapter 53, Matthew may be preparing us for what is to come in Section Six of his Gospel: Isaiah tells us that the Servant of the Lord will also take our *sins* on his shoulders (see my comments on chapter 20:28).

So this is who Jesus loves: outsiders. This should make us want to follow him.

But there is a price to pay.

Section Two: The Lord (Matthew 8:1 – 11:1) 55

B. Two warnings for disciples (8:18-22)

The attractiveness of Jesus could make some people think they want to sign up immediately to become his disciples. But these two warnings, in two men who want to follow Jesus, will encourage us to count the cost first.

1. – A man who claims too much (18-20)

This is a teacher of the law who is full of enthusiasm: *Teacher, I will follow you wherever you go* (19). This is a big claim.

In reply, Jesus says that *foxes have dens and birds have nests, but the Son of Man has nowhere to lay his head* (20). The fact that we read no more about this man suggests that he decides not to follow Jesus after all.

It is worth mentioning here that the phrase *Son of Man,* which Jesus sometimes uses to identify himself with the glorious Son of Man of Daniel 7:13-14, was also used in the first century as another way of referring to oneself (compare Matt 16:13 with Mark 8:27 for an example of this). This is what Jesus is doing here: he is saying *I have nowhere to lay my head.*

But the lesson is clear from this teacher of the law's encounter with Jesus: the decision to follow him is one that needs careful thought: am I willing to pay the price?

2. – A man who offers too little (21-22)

This man, who is described as already being a disciple (see 21), asks Jesus to *first let me go and bury my father* (21). The answer might sound harsh: Jesus tells him to *follow me, and let the dead bury their own dead* (22).

This man's father is almost certainly still alive: the funeral is a long way off. So Jesus is not telling the man he should not go to his father's funeral; rather he is telling him that putting off real discipleship until his father has died means that he is not willing for Jesus to take precedence over everything else.

The man had called Jesus *Lord* (21), which, as we have already seen (see chapter 8:2) may just mean *Sir*. But anyone who decides to follow Jesus must acknowledge his lordship in every area of life.

Jesus is telling us to count the cost.

C. Where Jesus is Lord (8:23 – 9:8)

In his second three-miracle block in Section Two, Matthew shows us Jesus' effortless authority in three areas in which human beings are powerless.

He is encouraging us to look at Jesus again.

1. – He rules nature (23-27)

Jesus is sleeping in the stern while the disciples are rowing across Lake Galilee. But then they are overwhelmed by *a furious storm (…) so that the waves swept over the boat* (24). The disciples are in a situation which is entirely outside of their control.

When they cry out to Jesus *Save us! We're going to drown!* (25) we hear desperation, but we hear faith too: they seem to believe that Jesus can rescue them.

You of little faith, why are you so afraid? Jesus asks them (26a). In other words, if they trusted him they wouldn't be filled with fear. Matthew tells us that Jesus *got up and rebuked the winds and the waves, and it was completely calm* (26b).

This is the authority of Jesus in action: he speaks to the weather, and the weather obeys. Jesus rules nature.

The disciples are astonished and ask one another *What kind of man is this? Even the winds and the waves obey him!* (27)

They don't yet know the answer, but they are asking the right question. This is the question Matthew wants us to be asking, too.

But there is more.

2. – He crushes evil (28-34)

Two demon-possessed men rush to meet Jesus as the boat arrives at the shore: *they were so violent that no one could pass that way* (28b).

The evil spirits controlling them know immediately who Jesus is: *What do you want with us, Son of God?* (29a) That they use the phrase *Son of God* means much more than that they recognise that Jesus is the Messiah: they see that he is in eternal relationship with God.

Their question to Jesus is fascinating: *Have you come here to torture us before the appointed time?* (29b) The evil spirits in these men know that there is an *appointed time* when evil will finally be vanquished for ever:

they are thinking of the Second Coming of Jesus the Son of God in glory at the end of history.

It's like they're saying to Jesus *You're early!*

Matthew tells the rest of the story quickly: The demons ask to be sent into the pigs; Jesus grants their request and drives the demons out of the men and into the pigs, which rush into the lake and drown. On hearing what has happened, *the whole town went out to meet Jesus* (34a).

In order to thank him? No, says Matthew: *they pleaded with him to leave their region* (34b). They want no contact with a man who possesses such authority.

Matthew doesn't tell us how these two men react to the freedom which Jesus has given them. But we can be sure that they, unlike the crowds, are glad to recognise Jesus' power over evil.

But there is a third area in which we see that Jesus is Lord.

3. – He forgives sin (9:1-8)

A paralysed man has been brought to Jesus by his friends. When Jesus sees their faith he says to the man *Take heart, son; your sins are forgiven* (2b).

Some teachers of the law are there and say to themselves *This fellow is blaspheming!* (3)

They are right, but only if Jesus is anything less than fully God. Only God has the right to forgive sin, because only God has no sins of his own. So there is no doubt about it: in claiming to have the right to forgive sin Jesus is claiming to be God.

Jesus knows what the teachers of the law are thinking (see 4a). So he asks them a question: *Which is easier: to say 'Your sins are forgiven,' or to say 'Get up and walk'?* (5)

The question is brilliant. Of course it's easier to *say* the sentence about forgiveness of sin, because no one will expect any physical evidence of something having happened: it is much harder to *say* to a paralysed man *Get up and walk,* because there needs to be some visible result.

So now, having already *said* the easier sentence (*Your sins are forgiven,* 2b), Jesus now says the harder one (*Get up, take your mat and go home,* 6b): when the miracle happens, people will know *that the Son of Man has authority on earth to forgive sins* (6a).

And that, says Matthew, is exactly what happens. The man is healed, thus proving that Jesus really has forgiven his sins (see 7).

The crowd are filled with awe: *they praised God, who had given such authority to men* (8b). They see that Jesus has authority to forgive sin, but they haven't yet drawn any conclusion from this.

But for those with the eyes to see it, the healing of the paralysed man proves that Jesus is none other than God himself.

We have watched as Jesus has ruled nature, cursed evil and forgiven sin. This must surely make us consider following him.

So Matthew tells us that that is just what he has done himself.

D. Two stories for disciples (9:9-17)

1. – Jesus calls Matthew and eats with sinners (9-13)

This is Matthew's Hitchcock moment.

Just as director Alfred Hitchcock appeared, however fleetingly, in all of his films, so Matthew includes the story in his Gospel of how Jesus called him to be a disciple. He describes himself as *a man named Matthew sitting at the tax collector's booth* (9a).

The first thing Matthew does is to invite Jesus and the other disciples to his house for a meal. But also on the guest-list are *many tax collectors and sinners* (10; that word *sinners* may be a euphemism for *prostitutes*).

The Pharisees are not happy about this and ask the disciples *Why does your teacher eat with tax collectors and sinners?* (11) In the first century, eating with people demonstrated love and acceptance; in their opinion this is disgraceful behaviour on Jesus' part.

But Jesus sees things differently. He replies that *it is not the healthy who need a doctor, but those who are ill* (12); and that *I have not come to call the righteous, but sinners* (13b). The message is clear: Jesus is claiming that he can cure people's sin problem.

But the impact of his words is all the stronger because of what Jesus quotes God as saying in the Old Testament prophecy of Hosea: *I desire mercy, not sacrifice* (13a, quoting Hosea 6:6). This is important because he tells the Pharisees to *go and learn what this means* (13a).

This is straight talking from Jesus. God had created the sacrificial system himself, so he was not dismissing it. But a slavish outward commitment to the rituals of worship was nothing if there was no mercy and compassion in the heart of the worshippers.

But this is Jesus the doctor's diagnosis of the spiritual state of the Pharisees.

This encounter is bound to increase the tension between Jesus and official first-century Judaism, a tension which will continue to grow throughout Matthew's Gospel.

2. – Jesus predicts a radical break with Judaism (14-17)

This second story for disciples is ostensibly about fasting: why do Jesus' disciples not fast (see 14)?

The real issue here, though, is that Jesus makes clear that his conflict with the religious leaders will only intensify.

He uses three pictures to explain the situation. The first is a wedding (see 15): while the bridegroom is present the guests are hardly going to fast! The second is the cloth (16): you don't repair an old piece of clothing with a patch of new material. And the third picture is the wine and the wineskins (17): new wine and old wineskins are a disastrous combination.

Jesus is referring to himself when he mentions the bridegroom in verse 15. In the Old Testament God himself is the bridegroom, never the Messiah; but here is Jesus calmly casting himself in the role.

It is significant, too, that *the bridegroom will be taken from them* (15), an almost violent expression which may be an allusion to the fourth Servant Song in the prophecy of Isaiah: *By oppression and judgment he was taken away* (Isa 53:8).

Jesus' comments about new wine and old wineskins are extremely provocative. The religious leaders are the old wineskins and Jesus himself is the new wine: they will not welcome and accept him. If you have new wine the only solution is to *pour new wine into new wineskins (17b)*.

Jesus is signalling a radical break with Judaism and flagging up the creation of a new community. Put at its simplest, the message is that Jesus and religion do not mix.

We have to choose.

E. What Jesus does (9:18-34)

Now Matthew introduces us to his last three-miracle block in Section Two. Of course these are historical events. But by ordering these in the way he does, Matthew is also telling us what Jesus still does today.

1. – He gives life (18-26)

This is actually a double miracle: while Jesus is on his way to the synagogue leader's house to raise his daughter from death, he heals a woman who is *subject to bleeding* (20).

But the message of both miracles is the same: Jesus gives life.

Because Matthew is in a hurry to make that point he shortens both stories (Mark's version is twice as long, see Mark 4:21-43). He misses out all unnecessary details so that he can focus our attention on what matters most.

The synagogue leader asks Jesus to come because his *daughter has just died* (18). The fact that he is a *synagogue leader* (18, 23) shows that what Jesus has just said (see 17) doesn't apply to *all* religious leaders: some *are* welcoming him and asking for his help.

So Jesus is going to give life to this girl and to her family.

But he does this for the woman with the bleeding, too. She has been experiencing a living death: because of her condition she is seriously ill, ritually unclean and desperately lonely. When she touches Jesus *the woman was healed at that moment* (22b).

Jesus gives life. But there is more.

2. – He opens eyes (27-31)

Despite their blindness, these two men *can* see something: Jesus is the *Son of David* (27). We have already seen that this is an expression used in the first century to refer to the promised Messiah (see my comments on chapter 1:1-17).

Jesus' question *Do you believe that I am able to do this?* (28) underlines the importance of faith (see also 22), as do his words as he performs the miracle: *According to your faith let it be done to you* (29).

Then, says Matthew, *their sight was restored* (30a).

The two men disobey Jesus' command not to tell anyone about their healing (see 30b-31). But the big thing here is that Jesus has opened their eyes.

My guess is that Matthew wants us to understand that Jesus is still doing that today. Sometimes he may do it physically; but, even more importantly, he does it spiritually as he opens the eyes of our hearts to see who he is.

That is a discovery which changes us for ever.

3. – He loosens tongues (32-34)

Matthew mentions that this man was possessed by an evil spirit but the emphasis is on the result: he *could not talk* (32). He does the same thing when recording the healing: *When the demon was driven out, the man who had been mute spoke* (33a).

Now Matthew tells us about how two groups of people react to the miracle. *The crowd was amazed* (33b), but the Pharisees conclude that *it is by the prince of demons that he drives out demons* (34). This second reaction is already an example of the old wineskins not being able to contain the new wine (see 17).

With his last three-miracle block, Matthew is preaching. As well as reporting historical events he is telling us what Jesus still does today: he gives life, he opens eyes and he loosens tongues.

Whenever someone gets to know Jesus they want to tell others. Which is the theme that Matthew turns to at the end of Section Two's narrative part.

F. Two facts for disciples (9:35-38)

This paragraph acts as a bridge between the narrative part and the teaching part of the section.

If Jesus had authority *then* to change all those people's lives in the events we've been reading about, then he still has authority *now*.

Matthew tells us that Jesus continues *teaching in their synagogues, proclaiming the good news of the kingdom and healing every disease and illness* (35). But now he wants us to know two facts.

1. – What Jesus feels (35-36)

When he saw the crowds, says Matthew, *he had compassion on them* (36a). Jesus' heart goes out to people who are *harassed and helpless, like sheep without a shepherd* (36b).

In the Old Testament prophecy of Ezekiel, God had promised that the Messianic shepherd would come to care for his people: *I will place over them one shepherd, my servant David, and he will tend them; he will tend them and be their shepherd* (Ezek 34:23).

Because the people don't recognise that that shepherd has come, Jesus *feels* something.

Compassion.

2. – What Jesus wants (37-38)

He wants his disciples to pray to *the Lord of the harvest* (38a): he is talking about himself.

The reason Jesus wants this is that *the harvest is plentiful but the workers are few* (37). There are many people, says Jesus, who are ready to respond, but not enough people to proclaim the message.

And so disciples need to *ask the Lord of the harvest, therefore, to send out workers into his harvest field* (38). Jesus followers must pray then – and now – that Jesus will give his disciples the desire to go and tell others about the shepherd.

Jesus is the Lord; and this is what he wants.

You might want to take a moment now to talk to Jesus about this: thank him that the harvest is his, and ask him to motivate more and more people to tell others about him and his kingdom.

We have seen it in the narrative part of Section Two: Jesus is worth talking about!

Teaching (10:1 – 11:1)

After they have seen the effortless authority of Jesus in action it is very likely that the disciples want to tell others about his kingdom, and to be the answer to their own prayer (see chapter 9:38).

So this teaching part of the section is on the subject of mission.

We need wisdom as we read this. Some of this is applicable for all disciples at all times, while other ingredients just apply to the Twelve.

A. Mission: its authority (10:1-4)

1. – Where it's from (1)

Matthew spells it out for us: after calling the disciples to him *he gave them authority to drive out impure spirits and to heal every disease and illness* (1).

Jesus is the source of the authority they now possess.

And it looks like this authority has no limits: they will not be able to heal in some cases only, but to heal *every* disease and illness.

2. – Who it's for (2-4)

Matthew uses a word here for the only time in his Gospel, when he tells us *the names of the twelve apostles* (2). The word means *sent ones* and is very appropriate because of what Jesus has in mind.

If Jesus had chosen eleven or thirteen apostles that would have been unremarkable. But the number *twelve* inevitably raises questions in our minds. We remember that Jesus has already signalled a radical break with traditional first-century Judaism (see chapter 8:14-17).

Now here he is, sending out twelve apostles. Are they to replace the twelve tribes of Israel and to be the foundation stone of a new people of God? Matthew doesn't answer the question here, but the theme will return dramatically in Section Five.

Of the twelve apostles, there are three who Matthew draws attention to. He begins his list with the words *first, Peter* (2): it looks like Peter is already being acknowledged as the leader of the Twelve. The last name on the list is *Judas Iscariot, who betrayed him* (4): the comment after the name is more than a hint of what is to come.

And the third apostle with an extra note attached is *Matthew the tax collector* (3): we are being reminded of his call in the narrative part of Section Two (see chapter 9:9-13). Matthew the Gospel-writer still refers to himself as *the tax collector*, although he has left his disreputable past behind him for something much more exciting.

So this is the group who receive authority from Jesus to go out in mission.

B. Mission: its description (10:5-15)

These twelve Jesus sent out, says Matthew (5a). The Lord of the harvest describes the mission to them.

1. – Proclamation to Jews, not Gentiles (5-6)

It is no surprise to hear that the apostles are to *go to the lost sheep of Israel* (6, and see my comments on chapter 9:36). Matthew began his Gospel by showing that Jesus was the Jewish Messiah (see chapter 1:1-17) and has underlined his fulfilment of Old Testament Scripture.

But it might seem strange that Jesus says *Do not go among the Gentiles or enter any town of the Samaritans* (5). Why does he need to say this? When a Jewish disciple was sent out in mission, would the idea of going to Gentiles with the message ever enter his mind?

Surely the answer must be Yes. Otherwise it makes no sense that Jesus forbids this. And they really might have decided to go to the Gentiles because they have already witnessed Jesus not only helping a Gentile centurion but predicting that many Gentiles will one day be part of God's kingdom (see chapter 8: 5-13).

But for now, says Jesus, the focus is to be on Jews alone.

2. – Proclamation in word and deed (7-8)

Jesus' disciples are to *proclaim this message: 'The kingdom of heaven has come near'* (7). This is the message that John the Baptist and Jesus himself have already preached (see chapter 3:2 and 4:17).

Now they are to pass it on. The messianic age is dawning, making it possible for people to come home to God.

But Jesus also tells his disciples to *heal those who are ill, raise the dead, cleanse those who have leprosy, drive out demons* (8a). They have already seen Jesus do those things himself (see chapter 8:16; 9:25; 8:3), and now such miracles are to be a part of their proclamation of the kingdom.

Of course we should ask God for miraculous works of power today, and sometimes he will answer our prayer. But it looks like the apostles, with the authority of Jesus at their disposal, are to expect such things to be happening often.

But let's not forget: when miracles happen today, it's *before the appointed time* (see chapter 8:29 and my comments there).

The principle still applies: we are to proclaim the kingdom of God not only with our words, but also with our actions. And our motivation, says Jesus, is clear: *Freely you have received; freely give* (8b).

3. – Proclamation while trusting God (9-15)

Jesus wants the disciples to be trusting not in their own resources, but in God's: *Do not get any gold or silver to take with you in your belts – no bag for the journey or extra shirt or sandals or a staff* (9-10a).

Hospitality was a part of first-century Jewish culture, so the command to find *some worthy person and stay at their house* (11) makes complete

Section Two: The Lord (Matthew 8:1 – 11:1)

sense: but, once again, the disciples are going to be trusting God that he will provide this. And *if the home is deserving,* says Jesus, *let your peace rest on it* (12a): this is a promise of a reward for all those who take Jesus disciples into their home.

But Jesus knows that his team will experience rejection, too: he talks about people who *will not welcome you or listen to your words* (14a). When that happens he tells them to *shake the dust off your feet* (14b) and to trust that God will remember this at the end of history: *It will be more bearable for Sodom and Gomorrah on the day of judgment than for that town* (15).

When disciples go out to proclaim Jesus and his kingdom we need to be trusting God and not ourselves.

C. Mission: its opposition (10:16-25)

Jesus has just talked about rejection. But now he drives the point home: he is *sending you out as sheep among wolves* (16a). But the reaction of the disciples to this danger is to be wise in their behaviour and to show integrity in their contact with others: *Be as shrewd as snakes and as innocent as doves* (16b).

Now Jesus explains what form the persecution is going to take.

1. – Arrest and trial (16-20)

The disciples can expect to be *handed over to the local councils and be flogged in the synagogues* (17). This will bring them into pressure situations: because of Jesus they will be *brought before governors and kings as witnesses to them and to the Gentiles* (18).

But when they stand trial they are not to worry about what to say in their defence: *At that time you will be given what to say* (19b). The disciples can count on God looking after them, *for it will not be you speaking, but the Spirit of your Father speaking through you* (20).

2. – Betrayal and hatred (21-23)

Jesus warns his friends that even family members will hand one another over to the authorities: *Brother will betray brother to death, and a father his child; children will rebel against their parents and have them put to death* (21).

So the message of Jesus and his kingdom will even divide families.

And the disciples will experience this rejection personally: they *will be hated by everyone because of me* (22a). But Jesus combines this warning with an encouragement to persevere, because *the one who stands firm to the end will be saved* (22b).

When persecuted the message-bringers are to move on to the next place (see 23a), because *you will not finish going through the towns of Israel before the Son of Man comes* (23b).

What does Jesus mean? There will never come a time when all Jews have heard the good news of the kingdom: there will always be more who still need to hear the message.

In talking about the day when *the Son of Man comes,* Jesus of course may be referring to his Second Coming at the end of human history. But it is more likely that the title *Son of Man* is pointing us to the Old Testament prophet Daniel, who had a vision of *one like a son of man coming with the clouds of heaven. He approached the Ancient of Days and was led into his presence* (see Dan 7:13).

This is not a coming *from* God, but a coming *to* God, which was fulfilled in the ascension and exaltation of Jesus after his resurrection. Until that day, says Jesus, the apostles will be telling their fellow-Jews about the Messiah.

And of course all people, Jewish people included, still need to hear the good news about Jesus.

3. – Being treated like Jesus (24-25)

Jesus rounds off this part of his teaching by telling the disciples that they should not be surprised by persecution: if they did it to Jesus it will happen to them too, because *the student is not above the teacher* (24a).

The head of the house, says Jesus, referring to himself, *has been called Beelzebul* (25), which is a name for Satan (see chapter 9:34; 12:24). Then the conclusion is obvious: *how much more the members of his own household!* (25b)

As they are sent out the disciples are under no illusions. Jesus has told them the truth: when they proclaim the good news there will be opposition.

But he will give them the resources they need.

D. Mission: its secret (10:26-42)

Being sent out in mission by Jesus is not going to be a stress-free experience: at times there will be fierce opposition. Now Jesus tells the disci-

Section Two: The Lord (Matthew 8:1 – 11:1)

ples truths which will prevent them getting knocked sideways when persecution comes.

It's like he's saying *The secret of dealing with the reality of opposition is to know these three things.*

1. – There is a Judgment Day (26-33)

Do not be afraid, says Jesus, *of those who kill the body but cannot kill the soul* (28a, see also 26a and 31a). The reason is that there is going to be a final reckoning one day, when *there is nothing concealed that will not be disclosed* (26).

Jesus urges his disciples *Rather, be afraid of the One who can destroy both soul and body in hell* (28b). He is talking about God, who will judge his enemies on Judgment Day and who, till then, will look after his children.

To explain what he means Jesus talks about sparrows, which cannot *fall to the ground outside your Father's care* (29b). Why should we ever be afraid, when God knows us so intimately that he even knows how many hairs we have on our heads (see 30)?

So don't be afraid, says Jesus: *you are worth more than many sparrows* (31).

So it's important that disciples remember the reality of Judgment Day. Those who acknowledge Jesus publicly he will also acknowledge *before my Father in heaven* (32b).

But this coin has two sides: *Whoever disowns me before others, I will disown before my Father in heaven* (33).

2. – This is part of the plan (34-36)

Opposition and persecution do not mean that everything has gone wrong: they are part of God's purpose.

Do not suppose that I have come to bring peace to the earth, says Jesus. *I did not come to bring peace, but a sword* (34). He quotes the prophecy of Micah in the Old Testament, and claims to fulfil these words: *A man's enemies will be the members of his own household* (36, quoting Micah 7:6).

Jesus knows that he and his message are divisive: some will accept him but others will reject him. This is part of God's plan.

3. – There are two responses (37-42)

First, in verses 37-39a, there is a negative response to Jesus.

Anyone who loves a family member more than they love Jesus *is not worthy of me* (37). Suffering is part of the discipleship deal, so that *whoever does not take up their cross and follow me is not worthy of me* (38).

If the focus of my life is me and my satisfaction, the inevitable will happen: I will *lose it (39a)*. But if I give my life to Jesus and his glory, I will *find it* (39b).

So second, in verses 39b-42, there is a positive response to Jesus.

Jesus makes the extraordinary promise here that *anyone who welcomes you welcomes me, and anyone who welcomes me welcomes the one who sent me* (40). And he says that people who give *even a cup of cold water to one of these little ones who is my disciple* (42) will be rewarded by God.

So there are two responses to Jesus: some will say *Yes* and others will say *No*.

If we remember the three things Jesus has taught us at the end of his teaching block on mission, we will be better equipped to cope with the ups and downs we experience as we proclaim him and his kingdom.

With that, Section Two has reached its conclusion. Matthew tells us as much: *After Jesus had finished instructing his twelve disciples...* (chapter 11:1). This signals that the section is over and that a new section is about to begin (compare chapter 7:28).

So, says Matthew, Jesus *went on from there to teach and preach in the towns of Galilee* (chapter 11:1b).

What happens next we will discover in Section Three.

Learning the Gospel

I hope you will take time to learn Section Two. Remember that this is not about learning every word but the order of the events.

Begin with the narrative part. Learn the headings in bold first: remember that three-miracle blocks alternate with blocks of two lessons for disciples.

When you have mastered the headings in bold, learn the sub-headings. This is not difficult because as you learn them, many of the details of every event will come back to you.

Section Two: The Lord (Matthew 8:1 – 11:1)

Then go on to the teaching part of the section: first learn the headings in bold, then the sub-headings.

Remember that it might help to agree with a friend that you will both learn the structure of Section Two. Remember, too, that as more and more of the section gets into your memory, the Holy Spirit will use it to *change* you.

There is power in the word of God!

Section Two: The Lord
Narrative

A. Who Jesus loves
  1. He heals a leper
  2. He heals a centurion's servant
  3. He heals Peter's mother-in-law

B. Two warnings for disciples
  1. A man who claims too much
  2. A man who offers too little

C. Where Jesus is Lord
  1. He rules nature
  2. He crushes evil
  3. He forgives sin

D. Two stories for disciples
  1. Jesus calls Matthew and eats with sinners
  2. Jesus predicts a radical break with Judaism

E. What Jesus does
  1. He gives life
  2. He opens eyes
  3. He loosens tongues

F. Two facts for disciples
  1. What Jesus feels
  2. What Jesus wants

Teaching

A. Mission: its authority
1. Where it's from
2. Who it's for

B. Mission: its description
1. Proclamation to Jews, not Gentiles
2. Proclamation in word and deed
3. Proclamation while trusting God

C. Mission: its opposition
1. Arrest and trial
2. Betrayal and hatred
3. Being treated like Jesus

D. Mission: its secret
1. There is a Judgment Day
2. This is part of the plan
3. There are two responses

'When Jesus had finished…'

Meeting the Lord

As you move through the ingredients of Section Two in your mind, tell yourself the story (with as many details as you can remember), or do this with a friend. As you do, keep responding to what you have been thinking by talking to Jesus.

You will be reminded of his authority and lordship as you watch him do miracles in the narrative part of the section: thank him for his power. And as, between the miracle-blocks, you see what Jesus says about discipleship, talk to him about your own life and ask him to help you follow him more passionately.

And when you start running through Jesus' teaching about mission, talk to him about your own hopes and fears when it comes to sharing the good news with others.

One of the main reasons God has given us Matthew's Gospel is so that we can encounter Jesus.

He is waiting to meet you.

Section Three: The Enemy
Matthew 11:2 – 13:53

In Section Two we saw Jesus the Lord healing and teaching with effortless authority, and the crowds reacting with enthusiasm. But there have also been hints that the religious leaders are far from pleased with the impact Jesus is having. Now, in Section Three, it becomes clear that they see him as the enemy: the Pharisees even make the decision that Jesus must be got rid of. But through it all, he continues to meet their objections and to proclaim the kingdom of God.

>Jesus told them many things in parables, saying:
>'A farmer went out to sow his seed.
>As he was scattering the seed,
>some fell along the path,
>and the birds came and ate it up.'
>
>Matthew 13:3-4

Enjoying the View

Narrative (11:2 – 12:50)

A. Three questions (11:2-19)
  1. A question about Jesus (2-6)
  2. A question about John (7-15)
  3. A question about the crowds (16-19)

B. Jesus: his message (11:20-30)
  1. Condemnation: a warning of judgment (20-24)
  2. Invitation: an offer of rest (25-30)

C. Three attacks (12:1-50)
  1. 'He's breaking the Sabbath' (1-21)
  2. 'He's working with Satan' (22-37)
  3. 'He should give us a sign' (38-45)

Teaching (13:1-53)

A. First parable: The sower (13:1-23)
  1. The puzzle (3-9)
  2. The reason (10-17)
  3. The explanation (18-23)

B. Three parables about growth (13:24-43)
  1. The weeds (24-30)
  2. The mustard seed (31-32)
  3. The yeast (33)
  4. The explanation of the parable of the weeds (36-43)

C. Three parables about response (13:44-50)
  1. The treasure (44)
  2. The pearl (45-46)
  3. The net (47-48)
  4. The explanation of the parable of the net (49-50)

D. Last parable: The householder (13:51-52)
'When Jesus had finished...' (13:53)

Section Three: The Enemy (Matthew 11:2 – 13:53)

Section Three's narrative part begins with three questions which show that there is a mixed response to Jesus and ends with three attacks by some of the religious leaders designed to distract him from his goals. Between these two units we see Jesus continuing to proclaim his message of judgment and love.

The teaching part of the section is a collection of eight of Jesus' parables. They explain why there is such opposition to Jesus: this will encourage disciples to continue to follow him and to share his message with others.

Before reading any further in this book, please read Section Three in Matthew's. As you do so, take time to think, to ask Jesus questions that occur to you, and to thank him for his determination to continue with his mission despite the opposition.

And please be expecting the Holy Spirit to be using what you read in your life: there is power in the word of God.

Unpacking the Content

Narrative (11:2 – 12:50)

Section Three begins with John the Baptist expressing doubts about Jesus. But the pressure increases: before we get to the end of the narrative part the religious leaders have decided to do away with him.

A. Three questions (11:2-19)

1. – A question about Jesus (2-6)

This is a question asked by John the Baptist, who has been in prison since chapter 4:12. It looks like he has been sure, ever since baptising Jesus, that he is the Messiah (see chapter 3:13-17).

But now he is having doubts.

So he sends some of his disciples to ask Jesus the question *Are you the one who is to come, or should we expect someone else?* (3)

John may be wondering if Jesus is the real thing because he remembers words from the Messiah's manifesto in the prophecy of Isaiah. It begins like this: *The Spirit of the Sovereign Lord is on me, because the Lord has anointed me to proclaim good news to the poor* (Isa 61:1a).

But look how it continues: *He has sent me to bind up the broken-hearted, to proclaim freedom for the captives and release from darkness for the prisoners* (Isa 61:1b).

Freedom for the captives and the prisoners? John, says Matthew, is *in prison* (2).

Jesus' response is to send a message back to John with a reminder of what is happening in his ministry: *the blind receive sight, the lame walk, those who have leprosy are cleansed, the deaf hear, the dead are raised, and the good news is proclaimed to the poor* (5).

And he adds an encouragement to John to keep trusting him: *Blessed is anyone who does not stumble on account of me* (6).

With his answer to John, Jesus is making it very clear that he is indeed the Messiah.

2. – A question about John (7-15)

Now Jesus asks the crowd a question about John the Baptist. When many of them went out into the desert when John was preaching and baptising, *what did you go out to see?* (8)

Jesus provides some wrong answers to the question: *a reed swayed by the wind* (7) and *a man dressed in fine clothes* (8).

His third answer is right, but it doesn't go far enough: *A prophet? Yes, I tell you, and more than a prophet* (9). By this Jesus probably means that John is the greatest of the prophets because he fulfils God's words to the Messiah through Malachi: *I will send my messenger ahead of you, who will prepare your way before you* (10, quoting Mal 3:1).

In other words Jesus is saying that John is the forerunner for the Messiah.

This means that no one has ever been *greater than John the Baptist* (11a). Yet John himself, says Jesus, preached about the kingdom's arrival but did not experience its reality, with the result that *whoever is least in the kingdom of heaven is greater than he* (11b). In other words, John belonged really to the old covenant, because *all the Prophets and the Law prophesied until John* (13).

Jesus puts the emphasis on John's greatness by saying that *he is the Elijah who was to come* (14). He means that John fulfils Old Testament expectation about the Messiah's forerunner (see Mal 4:5-6): John was an Elijah-figure, not literally Elijah returned to earth (see John 1:21 and Luke 1:17).

In answering his own question about John, Jesus has made two things very clear.

First, there has been opposition to the kingdom of God from the very beginning: *From the days of John the Baptist until now, the kingdom of heaven has been subjected to violence* (12a).

And second, Jesus is the Messiah.

3. – A question about the crowds (16-19)

This third question is asked by Jesus, too: *To what can I compare this generation?* (16a)

Using a picture of children playing a game of weddings and funerals (see 16b-17), Jesus says that the crowds, for the most part, are never satisfied. John the Baptist's asceticism and his message of judgment resulted in accusations of demon possession (see 18), while Jesus' time spent with tax collectors and sinners got him labelled *a glutton and a drunkard* (19).

As with the first two questions, Jesus is again underlining that he will inevitably meet with opposition. And there is more on its way.

But first Matthew reminds us of Jesus' message.

B. Jesus: his message (11:20-30)

Despite the religious leaders' decision to see him more and more as their enemy, Jesus continues to proclaim his message. It has two strands: judgment for those who reject Jesus and love for those who recognise and respond to him.

1. – Condemnation: a warning of judgment (20-24)

Matthew give us the diagnosis of the problem. Jesus, he says, *began to denounce the towns in which most of his miracles had been performed, because they did not repent* (20).

Many people in *Chorazin* and *Bethsaida* (21) and in *Capernaum* too (23) had seen the kinds of miracles we read about in Section Two, but have turned their backs on Jesus. This makes them ripe for judgment: *Woe to you..!* (21)

What makes them even more guilty is that their refusal to repent puts even Tyre and Sidon (21) and also Sodom (23) in the shade: *If the miracles that were performed in you had been performed in Tyre and Sidon, they would have repented long ago in sackcloth and ashes* (21b, see also 23b).

These three towns, infamous for their rejection of God (see Isa 23:1-5 and Gen 18:20), would have repented of their sin. But Chorazin, Bethsaida and Capernaum *did not repent* (20) and so face punishment on the day of judgment.

But Jesus' message is about more than judgment.

2. – Invitation: an offer of rest (25-30)

In this paragraph Matthew focuses the magnifying glass on Jesus, so that we learn things we would never otherwise know.

Matthew shows us three things about Jesus which will help us to respond to his offer.

First, *his joy* (25-26). This is extraordinary because we are being allowed to hear Jesus talking to his Father, who he calls *Lord of heaven and earth* (25).

We can sense Jesus' joy as he begins *I praise you, Father* (25a). He is grateful that the significance of his coming, though hidden from *the wise and learned* (25b), has been *revealed... to little children* (25b).

By *little children* Jesus means people who are not self-satisfied but who are open to receive God's revelation. It fills Jesus with joy that God loves to reveal him: *Yes, Father, for this is what you were pleased to do* (26).

Second, *his status* (27). Every phrase here should make our hearts beat faster. *All things have been committed to me by my Father,* says Jesus: not some things, but *all things*. And he adds that *no one knows the Son except the Father*: only God the Father knows Jesus completely and recognises that he is *the Son*.

This is talking about his divine status. Jesus is in unique relationship with God.

But there is more.

The only person who knows God the Father perfectly and intimately is Jesus: *No one knows the Father except the Son.* The sentence could have stopped there, but Jesus adds something which should make us catch our breath: no one knows the Father except the Son *and those to whom the Son chooses to reveal him* (27b).

We don't know God the Father completely of course; but if Jesus has opened our eyes we can say that we know God.

It would be good to take a few moments to thank Jesus and to worship him.

And third, *his invitation* **(28-30).** Jesus is talking to all those who know that they are *weary and burdened* (28): he offers to give them *rest for your souls* (29b, see also 28). The word could also be translated *relief.*

All they need to do to experience this rest is to *come to me,* says Jesus (28). Matthew surely wants us to understand that this offer applies not only to those who first heard Jesus say these words, but to anyone and everyone who hears the invitation.

Coming to Jesus means that we obey his command to *take my yoke upon you and learn from me* (29a). This is not a yoke which wears us down: it lifts us up because he is *gentle and humble in heart* (29).

Jesus ends by telling us that *my yoke is easy and my burden is light* (30). This is an offer to come to him, to talk to him, and to experience rest for our souls.

Jesus' invitation still stands today.

C. Three attacks (12:1-50)

Now the opposition to Jesus becomes more visible: the Pharisees, and later the teachers of the law, clearly see him as their enemy. This is not just negative talk *about* Jesus, these are attacks *to his face.*

1. – 'He's breaking the Sabbath' (1-21)

The Pharisees are watching: they notice that the disciples are eating ears of corn they have picked. But because of what day it is, they tell Jesus *Your disciples are doing what is unlawful on the Sabbath* (2).

Jesus' answer is robust. If David *entered the house of God, and he and his companions ate the consecrated bread* (4a), then Jesus can decide what is done on the Sabbath. The implication is clear: Jesus is greater than David.

But Jesus goes further. Everyone agrees that the priests on Sabbath duty in the temple desecrate the Sabbath and yet are innocent (5). Now, instead of *implying* his superiority Jesus says straight out that *something greater than the temple is here* (6). He can do what he chooses on the Sabbath.

Jesus is condemning the judgmental spirit of the Pharisees: *If you had known what these words mean, 'I desire mercy, not sacrifice,' you would not have condemned the innocent'* (7, quoting Hosea 6:6). This is blunt speaking. If the Pharisees understood the Bible they would not be so quick to write people off: they would see mercy as being more important than religious ritual.

To cap it all Jesus calls himself *the Lord of the Sabbath* (8). This is extremely provocative, because in the first century the Sabbath command was seen as more or less the most important: this was because, by watching people carefully, you could assess if they were keeping it.

But the Pharisees are still *looking for a reason to bring charges against Jesus* (10). Because there is *a man with a shrivelled hand* in the synagogue (10a) they ask Jesus *Is it lawful to heal on the Sabbath?* (10b)

In reply Jesus reminds them that it was permitted to rescue a sheep which had fallen into a pit on the Sabbath (see 11), before drawing the obvious conclusion: *How much more valuable is a person than a sheep!* (12a)

Jesus ends with a comment they can hardly disagree with: *Therefore it is lawful to do good on the Sabbath* (12b).

And now he turns from the Pharisees to the man everyone is focused on. When the man obeys Jesus by stretching out his hand, *it was completely restored, just as sound as the other* (13b).

Matthew tells us nothing about the reaction of the man and of the other people in the synagogue, but only about the decision the Pharisees make: after leaving, they *plotted how they might kill Jesus* (14).

The battle lines are drawn. Jesus is the enemy and must be done away with.

Before moving on to the Pharisees' second attack on Jesus, Matthew wants to tell us how Jesus responds to the opposition. He is aware of the plot against him (see 15). So when he heals *all who were ill* (15), *he warned them not to tell others about him* (16).

This prompts Matthew to give us another of his fulfilment quotations: *This was to fulfil what was spoken through the prophet Isaiah* (17; see also my comments on chapter 8:17). This is the longest Old Testament quotation in his Gospel, so it is obviously very important. It is not hard to see why.

Matthew quotes from the first Servant Song in the prophecy of Isaiah (see 18-21, quoting Isa 42:1-4). When he comes, God's servant *will not quarrel or cry out* (19a): when the religious leaders brand him as their enemy Jesus is not going to retaliate.

Two more things are worth noticing here. First, the quotation about God's servant ends with the prediction that *in his name the nations will put their hope* (21). It's like Matthew is reminding us, just after the broadside from the Pharisees, that *Gentiles* are going to trust Jesus.

The other thing to mention is that this is the second time that Matthew has quoted from one of the Servant Songs in the prophecy of Isaiah (see chapter 8:17). The fourth song will talk about the servant carrying the sin of others and being punished in their place (see Isa 53:4-6).

That is what Jesus will be doing when the Pharisees' plan to kill him comes to fruition. Matthew is pointing us to the cross. Although it is lawful to do good on the Sabbath (12b), the Pharisees have murder on their minds (14).

2. – 'He's working with Satan' (22-37)

This second attack on Jesus comes as a result of his healing *a demon-possessed man who was blind and mute... so that he could both talk and see* (22). What makes the attack urgent is that many people are wondering if Jesus might be the Messiah: *Could this be the Son of David?* (23b)

So the Pharisees conclude that *it is only by Beelzebul, the prince of demons, that this fellow drives out demons* (24, see also chapter 9:34, 10:25).

In reply Jesus asks them three questions.

First, isn't it ridiculous to suggest that Satan drives out Satan? (see 25-26)

Second, if exorcism is performed by other Jews, why should Jesus' driving out of demons be suspect? (see 27)

Jesus introduces his third question with a confident argument: *If it is by the Spirit of God that I drive out demons, then the kingdom of God has come upon you* (28). The Pharisees should be recognising the arrival of the kingdom in Jesus' works of power: but they are refusing to do this.

So now, with his third question, Jesus uses a parable to explain what is really happening when he drives out demons: *How can anyone enter a strong man's house and carry off his possessions unless he first ties up the strong man? Then he can plunder his house* (29).

Satan is the strong man and sinners are in his power as his possessions: what Jesus is doing is waging war on Satan by setting sinners free.

Matthew doesn't tell us if the Pharisees offered a reply to any of Jesus' questions. But it is unlikely that they did: they are unanswerable.

Jesus presses his point: *Whoever is not with me is against me* (30a). We have to make a decision: which side are we going to be on?

And now Jesus warns the Pharisees about the consequences of the decision they seem close to taking: *Blasphemy against the Spirit will not be forgiven* (31b, see also 32). They have seen plenty of evidence that Jesus is indeed the one fulfilling Old Testament prophecies about the coming Messiah; but they still choose to say that he is working with Satan.

It looks like Jesus is pleading with the Pharisees to repent. What they say and do shows what they are like on the inside, because *a tree is recognised by its fruit* (33b) and *the mouth speaks what the heart is full of* (34b). So he warns them that *everyone will have to give account on the day of judgment* (36).

But, instead of repenting, the Pharisees regroup and launch a third attack on Jesus.

3. – 'He should give us a sign' (38-45)

This time they are teaming up with the teachers of the law: *Teacher, we want to see a sign from you* (38).

This is not a genuine request. These are professional sceptics who have already made up their minds, so Jesus calls them *a wicked and adulterous generation* (39).

So Jesus refuses to give them a sign, except for one which will happen in the future: *As Jonah was three days and three nights in the belly of a huge fish, so the Son of Man will be three days and three nights in the heart of the earth* (40: *three days and three nights* is a Jewish idiom meaning *a period of two nights*).

Jesus is not saying that the story of Jonah is in some sense predicting his own resurrection. Instead he means that, just as Jonah's rescue from the fish was a confirmation of his call to be a prophet to the people of Nineveh, so his own resurrection will confirm Jesus' divine calling to be the saviour of the world.

And now Jesus returns to the reality of the day of judgment: he is warning the Pharisees and the teachers of the law.

The pagan *men of Nineveh* repented when Jonah preached, and so on that day they will condemn this generation, because *something greater than Jonah is here* (41).

In the same way, the pagan *Queen of the South* responded as she encountered Solomon's wisdom, and so will condemn this generation on judgment day, because *something greater than Solomon is here* (42).

The claim is staggering. Jesus is greater than the temple (6), greater than Jonah (41) and greater than Solomon (42). And yet his listeners refuse to embrace him.

There is one last warning here. In talking about an evil spirit driven out of a person but then taking up possession again because *it finds the house unoccupied* (44), Jesus is telling his opponents that genuine repentance and a new allegiance to him are essential.

At the end of his response to the third attack on him, Jesus is still begging his listeners to think again.

But the narrative part of Section Three is not quite finished (the teaching part clearly begins at the beginning of chapter 13). After all the opposition Jesus has been exposed to, we now read about something which is the *opposite* of opposition.

Matthew doesn't tell us why Jesus' mother and brothers are standing outside, wanting to speak to him (46b, but see Mark 3:21 and 31). Jesus asks the question *Who is my mother, and who are my brothers?* (48)

He answers the question himself, as he points to those who are following him: *Here are my mother and my brothers. For whoever does the will of my Father in heaven is my brother and sister and mother* (49b-50).

Jesus is not rejecting Mary and his family. What he *is* saying is that there is a tie which is even closer than that of physical family. Those who follow him are doing what God wants and are now in relationship with Jesus.

Why does Matthew tell us this incident now? It's like he's saying *The religious leaders wanted a sign, so here's one: while they have been treating Jesus as their enemy, others have been welcoming him as their friend.*

The Jesus family is growing and God's kingdom is spreading, as people have been responding to Jesus' call to *Come to me* (see chapter 11:28a).

Teaching (13:1-53)

After the disciples have seen the hostility of the religious leaders to Jesus, they may well be asking themselves why this is happening. Jesus explains this in the first of the parables he tells here.

A. First parable: The sower (13:1-23)

Jesus is determined to teach the crowds, so much so that he *got into a boat and sat in it, while all the people stood on the shore* (2). For the time being they are not going to be able to ask for miracles: they are listening to Jesus.

1. – The puzzle (3-9)

The word *parable* can also mean *puzzle*: so when Matthew writes that Jesus *told them many things in parables* (3a), that can mean that he taught *enigmatically*.

So, says Jesus, *a farmer went out to sow his seed* (3b). The seed falls on four kinds of ground: *on the path, and the birds came and ate it up* (4), *on rocky places* (5), *but when the sun came up, the plants were scorched, and they withered because they had no root* (6), *among thorns which grew up and choked the plants* (7), and *on good soil, where it produced a crop* (8).

Would we have understood the meaning of the story? The only clues are the context and the ending.

In the context it makes sense for Jesus to talk about different reactions to his message: in the narrative part of Section Three we have seen the religious leaders treating him as their enemy.

And Jesus ends the parable by saying *Whoever has ears, let them hear* (9). Could that be a clue that the story is about how we listen to Jesus teaching the word of God?

2. – The reason (10-17)

Before we hear Jesus explaining his parable, Matthew tells us that the disciples ask him *Why do you speak to the people in parables?* (10)

The reason, says Jesus, is that *the knowledge of the secrets of the kingdom has been given to you, but not to them* (11). So there are two groups of people: some who don't understand and so reject God's message, and others who may not understand but who ask Jesus to help them (see 10, 36).

So the parables are not an intelligence test but an openness test, designed to show to which group each listener belongs. Spiritually open people are hungry to know more and so ask Jesus for help. This is still true today.

So important is this principle that we learn more about each group.

Of the first group, Jesus says *Whoever does not have, even what they have will be taken from them* (12b). He goes on to say that the reaction of the rejectors fulfils the prophecy of Isaiah: *You will be ever hearing but never understanding; you will be ever seeing but never perceiving* (14, quoting Isaiah 6:9-10).

But Jesus also talks about those people who, like the disciples, ask Jesus for help: *Whoever has will be given more, and they will have an abundance* (12a). And these people are no better than the other group, because what they understand is a result of blessing from God: *Blessed are your eyes because they see, and your ears because they hear* (16, see also 17).

The principle is clear: *Light received brings more light, while light rejected brings night.*

And the parables reveal that principle in action.

3. – The solution (18-23)

And now Jesus explains his parable-puzzle to the disciples. The seed is *the message about the kingdom* (19a), and the four different kinds of ground where the seed lands are four different kinds of human heart.

So there are hard hearts, where *the evil one comes and snatches away what was sown* (19); there are superficial hearts, when after initial enthusiasm people reject the message *since they have no root* (20-21); there are overfull hearts, where *the worries of this life and the deceitfulness of wealth choke the word* (22).

And then there are open hearts, which refers to *someone who hears the word and understands it* (23).

The parable of the sower explains to disciples why not everyone responds positively to Jesus and his message. Although there are four different reactions outlined here, in the last analysis there are are only two.

We are for Jesus or we are against him (see chapter 10:37-42 and 12:30).

B. Three parables about growth (13:24-43)

Now Jesus turns to more kingdom parables. He tells us three and explains the first of them.

1. – The weeds (24-30)

This story is about *a man who sowed good seed in his field* (24), and about his enemy who *came and sowed weeds among the wheat* (25).

When the man's servants ask him where the weeds come from, the reply is clear: *An enemy did this* (28a).

Asked if they should pull up the weeds, the man says No, because *while you are pulling up the weeds, you may uproot the wheat with them* (29). So he adds *Let both grow together until the harvest* (30a).

And at harvest time the man will tell the harvesters to *first collect the weeds and tie them in bundles to be burned; then gather the wheat and bring it into my barn* (30b).

The disciples haven't understood the parable (see 36), but can't ask Jesus for help until he has told two more.

2. – The mustard seed (31-32)

There was a proverb about the mustard seed being incredibly small, and yet *when it grows, it is the largest of garden plants and becomes a tree* (32).

That, says Jesus, is what *the kingdom of heaven is like* (31). It starts with one man and his message, but it will grow into something huge.

And there may even be a hint of that in Jesus' comment that the mustard tree is so big *that the birds come and perch in its branches* (32b). The Old Testament sometimes uses a tree as an image for a great empire (eg Dan 4:10-12), with the birds in its branches being the nations under the empire's protection (see Dan 4:20-22).

Is Jesus talking about the Gentiles coming into the kingdom of heaven? In any case the lesson from the mustard seed is clear: unspectacular beginnings lead to a triumphant climax.

But now Jesus tells another parable.

3. – The yeast (33)

A woman mixes some yeast *into about thirty kilograms of flour until it worked all through the dough* (33): this would make enough bread for a meal for a hundred people.

This is also what *the kingdom of heaven is like* (33): there will be extraordinary growth. Disciples, who might be unnerved by the opposition to Jesus, need to hear this message.

Matthew spells it out: *Jesus spoke all these things to the crowd in parables* (34a); indeed, *he did not say anything to them without using a parable* (34b).

This is important to Matthew because he is going to use another of his formula quotations: *So was fulfilled what was spoken through the prophet: 'I will open my mouth in parables, I will utter things hidden since the creation of the world'* (35, quoting Ps 78:2; see my comments on chapter 8:17).

Now, having heard Jesus' three parables about growth, the disciples at last have the opportunity to ask him to explain one of them.

4. – The explanation of the parable of the weeds (36-43)

The disciples come straight to the point: they want Jesus to *explain to us the parable of the weeds in the field* (36b, see 24-30).

Jesus holds nothing back: *The one who sowed the good seed is the Son of Man. The field is the world, and the good seed stands for the people of the kingdom. The weeds are the people of the evil one, and the enemy who sows them is the devil* (37-39a).

And, says Jesus, *the harvest is the end of the age, and the harvesters are angels* (39b).

The rest of Jesus' explanation is a description of judgment day at the end of human history (see also 49-50 and chapter 25:31-46): *The Son of Man will send out his angels, and they will weed out of his kingdom everything that causes sin and all who do evil. They will throw them into the blazing furnace, where there will be weeping and gnashing of teeth* (41-42).

But there are great things in store for those who have trusted and followed Jesus: *the righteous will shine like the sun in the kingdom of their Father* (43a).

We are not told how the disciples reacted to Jesus' explanation, though surely they must have understood it. Jesus says again that *whoever has ears, let them hear* (43b).

But this doesn't mean that he has finished: he has more to say.

C. Three parables about response (13:44-50)

We have heard Jesus tell three parables about growth and explain one of them; now he tells three parables about response and explains one of them, too.

They answer two important questions the disciples might well have. What is the right response to Jesus and the message of the kingdom? And, however we choose to respond, what are the consequences?

1. – The treasure (44)

After finding treasure in a field and burying it again, a man *in his joy went and sold all he had and bought that field* (44).

What this man has found is so wonderful that anything he gives up is a small price to pay for the joy he is experiencing.

When we discover Jesus we realise that nothing is as important as knowing him. There is no joy like it.

2. – The pearl (45-46)

When a merchant finds an incredibly valuable pearl, *he went away and sold everything he had and bought it* (46).

He only goes to these extreme lengths because he recognises how precious the pearl is.

The message of the first two parables in this block might remind us of the words of Jim Elliot, who was martyred in 1956 when he tried to bring the gospel to the Auca Indians: *He is no fool who gives up what he cannot keep to gain what he cannot lose.*

But Jesus has a third parable.

3. – The net (47-48)

This story has a great deal in common with the parable of the weeds (see 24-30): Jesus is clearly wanting to drive his point home.

The huge fishing net is full, so the fishermen *collected the good fish in baskets, but threw the bad away* (48b).

Will the disciples have got the message because they have already had the parable of the weeds explained to them (see 36-43)?

Jesus is not leaving that to chance.

4. – The explanation of the parable of the net (49-50)

This is how it will be at the end of the age, says Jesus (49a). *The angels will come and separate the wicked from the righteous and throw them into the blazing furnace, where there will be weeping and gnashing of teeth* (49b-50).

The explanation is blunt and clear: on Judgment Day there will be a division.

Surely Jesus is wanting us to see how important it is that we respond rightly to him and the message of the kingdom.

The consequences are eternal.

D. Last parable: The householder (13:51-52)

Jesus wants to be sure that the disciples have really grasped the teaching he has given to them and not to the crowds, so asks *Have you understood all these things?* (51a)

When they reply that they have (see 51b), he tells them a final parable.

Section Three: The Enemy (Matthew 11:2 – 13:53)

What does Jesus mean when he talks about *every teacher of the law who has become a disciple in the kingdom of heaven* (52a)? He is not talking about official Jewish scribes, but about anyone who has known the Old Testament Scriptures but has then started to follow him.

So this includes the disciples who are listening.

Such a person, says Jesus, is *like the owner of a house who brings out of his storeroom new treasures as well as old* (52b).

The disciples knew Old Testament treasures before they met Jesus; through meeting him they have received new treasures. All these treasures are now in the storeroom of their minds.

Their task, says Jesus, is to *bring out* all these treasures and pass them on to others.

Which is what Matthew is doing for us.

We have reached the end of Section Three, as Matthew makes clear with his conclusion phrase: *When Jesus had finished...* (53a, see also chapter 7:28 and 11:1). Now, after Jesus has told his parables, *he moved on from there* (53b).

I don't know about you, but this makes me want to read Section Four. But before looking forwards, let's look back.

Learning the Gospel

I hope you see the value of learning Section Three: it is a great thing to have all these events in one's storeroom (see chapter 13:52), ready to share with others!

Begin with the narrative part and learn the headings in bold first. (And remember that doing this out loud will make it easier and quicker.)

Then learn the sub-headings: as you do so you will be surprised by how many of the details you will find yourself remembering.

Only when you have the narrative part committed to memory, move on to the parables in the teaching part. Once again, learn the headings in bold first, and then the sub-headings.

You will find it a help to have arranged with a friend that both of you will do this.

It won't take you long to learn Section Three, as it's quite short. If you run it through your mind once or twice a day, it will soon be in your long-term memory.

Section Three: The Enemy

Narrative

A. Three questions
1. A question about Jesus
2. A question about John
3. A question about the crowds

B. Jesus: his message
1. Condemnation: a warning of judgment
2. Invitation: an offer of rest

C. Three attacks
1. 'He's breaking the Sabbath'
2. 'He's working with Satan'
3. 'He should give us a sign'

Teaching

A. First parable: The sower
1. The puzzle
2. The reason
3. The explanation

B. Three parables about growth
1. The weeds
2. The mustard seed
3. The yeast
4. The explanation of the parable of the weeds

C. Three parables about response
1. The treasure
2. The pearl
3. The net
4. The explanation of the parable of the net

D. Last parable: The householder

'When Jesus had finished…'

Section Three: The Enemy (Matthew 11:2 – 13:53)

Meeting the Lord

Please remember that Matthew's Gospel is not only there so we can have information about Jesus: it is also there so we can meet him.

Begin telling yourself (or the friend you are doing this with) the account of the three questions at the start of the section, including as many details as you can.

As you re-tell the Jesus message of condemnation and invitation, take the opportunity to thank him for what he says. Ask Jesus to help you shoulder his yoke and to let you experience his offer of rest.

You will only be able to remember a few of the details as the religious authorities start their attack: but do what you can, and talk to Jesus.

Then re-tell the parables in the teaching part of the section: you will find yourself asking Jesus to make the kingdom grow more and more as he helps people to respond to him and his message. Take time to pray for friends who are not yet believers in Jesus.

And all the while, the Holy Spirit will be using his word in your life. As you re-tell Matthew you will be rediscovering Jesus.

Section Four: The Son
Matthew 13:54 – 19:2

Although the opposition has been increasing, Jesus has continued to proclaim the good news of the kingdom. Now, in Section Four, the focus is once more on Jesus, as he reveals himself to be the Son of God in eternal relationship with the Father. When Peter and the other disciples recognise this, he begins to tell them about his suffering and death.

> Whoever wants to be my disciple
> must deny themselves
> and take up their cross
> and follow me.
>
> Matthew 16:24

Section Four: The Son (Matthew 13:54 – 19:2)

Enjoying the View

Narrative (13:54 – 17:27)

A. Jesus: the authority he demonstrates (13:54 – 14:36)
1. Opposition in Nazareth (13:54-58)
2. The death of John the Baptist (14:1-12)
3. Feeding of the 5,000 (14:13-21)
4. Jesus walks on the water (14:22-33)
5. Healings in Gennesaret (14:34-36)

B. A double warning for disciples (15:1-20)
1. God's word and human tradition (1-9)
2. What makes people unclean? (10-20)

C. Jesus: the responses he gets (15:21 – 16:12)
1. Jesus and the Canaanite woman (15:21-28)
2. Jesus heals many Gentiles (15:29-31)
3. Feeding of the 4,000 (15:32-39)
4. The Pharisees and the Sadducees demand a sign (16:1-4)
5. The confusion of the disciples (16:5-12)

D. A double revelation for disciples (16:13-23)
1. Peter's confession of Jesus (13-20)
2. Jesus' first prediction (21-23)

E. Jesus: the disciples he wants (16:24 – 17:27)
1. The call to discipleship (16:24-28)
2. The transfiguration (17:1-13)
3. Jesus drives out an evil spirit (17:14-20)
4. Jesus' second prediction (17:22-23)
5. Paying the temple tax (17:24-27)

Teaching (18:1 – 19:2)

A. Be small (18:1-5)
1. Becoming like a little child (2-4)
2. Welcoming a little child (5)

B. Be careful (18:6-9)
1. Causing others to stumble (6-7)
2. Causing myself to stumble (8-9)

C. Be caring (18:10-14)
1. Respecting little ones (10)
2. Rescuing little ones (12-14)

D. Be discreet (18:15-20)
1. Step One (15)
2. Step Two (16)
3. Step Three (17-20)

E. Be forgiving (18:21-35)
1. Peter's question (21-22)
2. Jesus' parable (23-34)
3. Our responsibility (35)

'When Jesus had finished…' (19:1-2)

Matthew has done what he always does: he has divided the section into a narrative part and a teaching part.

The narrative part consists of three groups of five events (A, C and E), interspersed with a double warning (B) and a double revelation (D): the focus is on Jesus revealing his identity as the Son of God.

The teaching part of the section is about life in the new community Jesus is bringing into being. It answers this important question: How are disciples to relate to one another?

This is a long section. Please take time to read through Matthew's account from chapter 13:54 to chapter 19:2. As you do, take the opportunity to stop and to talk to Jesus: ask him questions and give him your heart.

Unpacking the Content

Narrative (13:54 – 17:27)

A. Jesus: the authority he demonstrates (13:54 – 14:36)

As we see Jesus in action we see his complete control of every situation.

Section Four: The Son (Matthew 13:54 – 19:2)

1. – Opposition in Nazareth (13:54-58)

Mattthew tells us that Jesus comes to *his home town* and teaches the people *in their synagogue* (54a): is he hinting that a Jewish meeting place is already starting to feel like foreign territory?

The people *were amazed* (54a), but they *took offence at him* (57a): they are sceptical because they know Jesus, they know his mother Mary and they know his brothers and sisters (see 55-56a).

Two of the questions they ask are especially interesting.

First, they wonder *Where did this man get this wisdom and these miraculous powers?* (54b) Jesus' authority is not in doubt; what they don't know is where he gets it from.

Second, they ask one another *Isn't this the carpenter's son?* (55a)

Because we have read Matthew's Introduction we know that the answer to that second question is *No* (see chapter 1:18, 20, 23): Jesus is not Joseph's son, but God's.

Jesus replies that *a prophet is not without honour except in his own town and in his own home* (57b). And Matthew adds that *he did not do many miracles there because of their lack of faith* (58).

But already, at the beginning of Section Four, we are being encouraged to remember whose son Jesus is.

2. – The death of John the Baptist (14:1-12)

Herod the tetrarch is sure about who Jesus is: *This is John the Baptist; he has risen from the dead!* (2a)

Matthew has already told us that John has been put in prison (see chapter 4:12); now we learn how that came about and what resulted.

John had preached against Herod for taking his brother's wife Herodias. For Herod, locking John up was second choice, because *he wanted to kill John, but he was afraid of the people, because they considered John a prophet* (5).

When Herodias' daughter dances at his birthday party Herod offers her anything she wants. She replies *Give me here on a dish the head of John the Baptist* (8), an answer her mother has put her up to.

The king was distressed, says Matthew, but grants her request *because of his oaths and his dinner guests* (9). It looks like Herod doesn't want to kill John after all, but he doesn't want to lose face by going back on his word.

After John has been executed and buried, John's disciples make a decision: *they went and told Jesus* (12b).

So Jesus knows that the pressure is continuing to build (see also 13a). But, as we shall see, he is determined to reveal his identity to the disciples and to the crowds.

3. – Feeding of the 5,000 (14:13-21)

When Jesus sees the crowds, *he had compassion on them and healed those who were ill* (14). Once again, his authority is there for all to see.

But something even more extraordinary is about to happen.

This is the only miracle of Jesus which is recorded by all four Gospel-writers; in addition Matthew and Mark tell us about the feeding of the 4,000. What is so important about Jesus feeding a huge crowd?

The answer may be in an Old Testament prophecy. In a poetic description of what we might call heaven, Isaiah writes: *On this mountain the Lord Almighty will prepare a feast of rich food for all peoples, a banquet of aged wine – the best of meats and the finest of wines. On this mountain he will destroy the shroud that enfolds all peoples, the sheet that covers all nations; he will swallow up death for ever. The Sovereign Lord will wipe away the tears from all faces; he will remove his people's disgrace from all the earth. The Lord has spoken* (Isa 25:6-8).

In the first century Jews referred to this celebration as *the messianic banquet*: they believed that the host at this feast at the end of time would be the Messiah (see also chapter 8:11). And now here is Jesus inviting 5,000 people to a meal.

Could this be a preview of the messianic banquet? If it is, that would make Jesus the Messiah.

So here is the crowd: *five thousand men, besides women and children* (21).

Matthew tells the story quickly. When the disciples urge Jesus to send the people away he puts them on the back foot by replying *You give them something to eat* (16b).

But the disciples have *only five loaves of bread and two fish* (17).

Now Jesus gives thanks to God for the food and hands it to the disciples for them to pass on to the crowds. Matthew tells us (but this must been after some considerable time) that *they all ate and were satisfied* (20a).

And there is lots left over: *the disciples picked up twelve basketfuls of broken pieces* (20b). There is more food *after* the meal than there was *before* it!

Section Four: The Son (Matthew 13:54 – 19:2)

This miracle points to the identity of Jesus: he is the promised Messiah.

4. – Jesus walks on the water (14:22-33)

Jesus made the disciples get into the boat and go on ahead of him to the other side (22a). It looks like he leaves them no choice: what he is about to do is so important.

Later that night the disciples are in the middle of the lake, their boat *buffetted by the waves because the wind was against it* (24b). This is not a storm, but the disciples certainly have their work cut out to make progress.

And now comes an astonishing experience for the disciples: *Shortly before dawn Jesus went out to them, walking on the lake* (25). He has suspended the downward pull of gravity. This is authority in action.

The disciples, understandably, are terrified: they think this is a ghost. So they *cried out in fear* (26b).

Of the four Gospel-writers only Matthew tells us about Peter's request to walk to Jesus on the water: *Then Peter got down out of the boat, walked on the water and came towards Jesus* (29).

But then the enormity of what he is doing overwhelms him: *When he saw the wind, he was afraid* (30a) and begins to sink.

When Jesus reaches out his hand to rescue Peter, he says to him *You of little faith, (…) why did you doubt?* (31b)

The wind dies down as Jesus and Peter climb back into the boat. But now Matthew records the biggest miracle of all: *Then those who were in the boat worshipped him, saying, 'Truly you are the Son of God'* (33).

Have they got it? Only God can walk on water (see also Job 9:8); and Jesus is God's eternal Son.

5. – Healings in Gennesaret (14:34-36)

When the boat reaches shore *people brought all who were ill to him* (35b) and ask Jesus to allow their friends to touch his cloak.

Matthew tells us that *all who touched it were healed* (36b; see also chapter 9:20-22).

As we look back on these five incidents we see Jesus demonstrating his authority. He is determined to reveal his identity: he is the Messiah and the Son of God.

And by telling us what happened in Gennesaret, Matthew may be encouraging us, his readers, to reach out *our* hands and touch Jesus for ourselves.

B. A double warning for disciples (15:1-20)

As the disciples watch Jesus interacting with some religious leaders they are thinking about what they hear (see 12 and 14). The two issues Jesus addresses are a warning for them.

1. – God's word and human tradition (1-9)

Some Pharisees and teachers of the law come to Jesus *from Jerusalem* (1), which suggests that they are on a special mission. They launch straight in with a question for Jesus: *Why do your disciples break the tradition of the elders? They don't wash their hands before they eat!* (2)

For first-century Jews there were two sources of revelation: the written word of God and the elders' tradition handed down through the years. Jesus' reply will show that the latter consists of *merely human rules* (9b).

The example he uses is the biblical command to *honour your father and mother* (4a). But the tradition said that when someone called their money *devoted to God* (5b), they didn't need to use this to help their parents.

Jesus makes his point twice over.

First, with a question: *Why do you break the command of God for the sake of your tradition?* (3)

And, second, with a statement: *Thus you nullify the word of God for the sake of your tradition* (6b).

This is strong language. It's like the religious leaders are saying that the Jewish Scriptures are of no value.

But Jesus goes further. He quotes from the Scriptures they claim to honour, arguing that Isaiah's description of God's people also applies to the leaders of Israel now:

> *These people honour me with their lips,*
> *but their hearts are far from me.*
> *They worship me in vain;*
> *their teachings are merely human rules.*
>
> (8-9, quoting Isa 29:13)

And so Jesus says to them *You hypocrites!* (7a)

Section Four: The Son (Matthew 13:54 – 19:2)   97

2. – What makes people unclean? (10-20)

Jesus is teaching the crowd now (see 10). What defiles a person in God's sight, he says, is not *what goes into someone's mouth* but rather *what comes out of their mouth* (11).

The disciples want to keep Jesus informed: *Do you know that the Pharisees were offended when they heard this?* (12)

But Jesus is not going to back down. He tells his disciples that the Pharisees are not in relationship with God: *Every plant that my heavenly Father has not planted will be pulled up by the roots* (13). This is close to what John the Baptist had said back in Section One of the Gospel (see chapter 3:7-10).

Jesus warns the disciples not to be on the Pharisees' side, because *they are blind guides* (14). To follow them will lead to disaster: *If the blind lead the blind, both will fall into a pit* (14b).

And now Jesus returns to the issue of what makes a person unclean in God's sight. He explains to the disciples that *the things that come out of a person's mouth come from the heart, and these defile them* (18).

Jesus is claiming that all these sins are to be found in the human heart: *murder, adultery, sexual immorality, theft, false testimony, slander. These are what defile a person* (19b-20a).

And Matthew makes it clear that these two warnings belong together by allowing us, now, to hear Jesus go back to the topic of Jewish tradition: *Eating with unwashed hands does not defile them* (20b).

These two incidents show us unmistakeably that Jesus is on a collision course with the leaders of Israel. And, at the same time, he's training his disciples.

C. Jesus: the responses he gets (15:21 – 16:12)

In this second block of five incidents we will see Jesus interacting with Gentiles, with the religious leaders and with the disciples. The responses are varied.

It's like Matthew is asking us *How are you responding to Jesus?*

1. – Jesus and the Canaanite woman (15:21-28)

The disciples have already seen Jesus reaching out to Gentiles (see chapter 8:5-13). Now he goes deliberately *to the region of Tyre and Sidon* (21).

A Canaanite woman starts calling out *Lord, Son of David, have mercy on me!* (22b): her daughter is demon-possessed. Does she call Jesus *Son of David* because she has heard that he is the Jewish Messiah?

When Jesus doesn't reply the disciples presumably think they are saying what he is thinking when they ask him to *send her away, for she keeps crying out after us* (23).

Jesus' answer is short and to the point: *I was sent only to the lost sheep of Israel* (24).

When the woman keeps asking for help Jesus tells her that *it is not right to take the children's bread and toss it to the dogs* (26). The word *dogs* was used as a Jewish term of abuse for Gentiles: it's almost like Jesus is identifying himself with the attitude behind it.

The woman's answer *Even the dogs eat the crumbs that fall from their master's table* (27) is astonishing, and it astonishes Jesus too: *Woman, you have great faith!* (28a, and see also chapter 8:10)

And her daughter is set free from the demon.

Two more things need to be said here, one about the woman and the other about Jesus.

Three times this Gentile woman has addressed Jesus as *Lord* (22,25,27). Often, as we have seen, this is equivalent to calling someone *Sir*; but it looks like this woman is acknowledging Jesus as someone with authority (compare the parallel passage in Mark 7:28, where she is the only person in Mark's Gospel who calls Jesus *Lord*).

And what do we make of Jesus' statement that he was *sent only to the lost sheep of Israel* (24)? Some people consider this to be little short of racism. But we have already seen that Jesus loves Gentiles (see chapter 8:5-13), and we have seen his joy at the Canaanite woman's faith (see 28).

It all makes much more sense when we recognise that there is a difference between Jesus being sent *to* the lost sheep of Israel and his being sent *for* the lost sheep of Israel.

God the Father sent Jesus to be the Saviour *for* everyone – Jews and Gentiles. But his priority while here physically in our world was the people of Israel: so he was *sent only to the lost sheep of Israel* (24).

But, as we are about to see, Jesus is here *for* Gentiles too.

2. – Jesus heals many Gentiles (15:29-31)

Jesus is in demand: Matthew tells us that *great crowds came to him, bringing the lame, the blind, the crippled, the mute and many others* (30a).

Section Four: The Son (Matthew 13:54 – 19:2) 99

What happens is extraordinary: *he healed them* (30b). And these are Gentiles.

What makes this clear is that their amazement at what Jesus is doing is followed by Matthew telling us that *they praised the God of Israel* (31b).

The phrase *the God of Israel* means that these people are themselves not part of Israel. They are astonished that Israel's God loves Gentiles too and amazed by the authority of Jesus in healing so many.

We are watching Gentiles responding to what Jesus is doing.

3. – Feeding of the 4,000 (15:32-39)

If this miracle, like the feeding of the 5,000 near the beginning of the section (see chapter 14:13-21) is a preview of the messianic banquet, it is particularly significant because the people here are Gentiles.

First-century Jews, for the most part, assumed that the banquet would be for Israel alone, and yet the prophecy from Isaiah mentioned earlier had promised *a feast of rich food for all peoples* (Isa 25:6).

Jesus tells his disciples that he feels *compassion for these people* (32, and see chapter 9:36) and thinks they should be fed. He underlines the impossibility of the situation by asking them how much food they have (see 34).

After the disciples have distributed the seven loaves and a few fish to these *four thousand men, besides women and children* (38), Matthew tells us that *they all ate and were satisfied. Afterwards the disciples picked up seven basketfuls of broken pieces that were left over* (37).

If we are surprised that the disciples seem to have forgotten that Jesus had fed 5,000 people (see 33), we will see in a moment that Jesus is surprised too at how slow they are to grasp the truth.

Despite what they have said in the boat after seeing him walking on the lake (see chapter 14:33), the disciples are still having trouble responding to Jesus by trusting him.

4. – The Pharisees and the Sadducees demand a sign (16:1-4)

The Pharisees and the Sadducees were two groups bitterly opposed to each other, but they are teaming up here to attack Jesus. They want *a sign from heaven* (1b).

People who demand signs, says Jesus, are *a wicked and adulterous generation* (4a). With his words in verses 2 and 3 he is telling them to open their eyes and look at the evidence they already have: they can forecast the weather, but *you cannot interpret the signs of the times* (3b).

The only thing Jesus is willing to give his opponents is *the sign of Jonah* (4b). Jesus has already explained what this means (see my comments on chapter 12:40-41): just as Jonah escaped after being swallowed by the large fish, the final evidence of Jesus' identity will be provided by his own resurrection from the dead.

Matthew adds that *Jesus then left them and went away* (4b). Obviously this is meant literally, but there may be a deeper meaning here, too.

The hard hearts of the religious elite are building a chasm between them and Jesus.

5. – The confusion of the disciples (16:5-12)

On their way across Lake Galilee, Jesus warns the disciples to watch out for *the yeast of the Pharisees and Sadducees* (6). But they start discussing who forgot the bread (see 5,7).

So Jesus reminds them about the feedings of the 5,000 and the 4,000 (see 9-10): presumably remembering that they have witnessed Jesus performing these two miracles should make them realise who he is.

They seem to have forgotten recognising Jesus to be the Son of God after he had walked on the water (see chapter 14:33); they are not yet confident about the identity of Jesus.

But they do at least now understand, says Matthew, that his comment about yeast was a warning about *the teaching of the Pharisees and Sadducees* (12b).

The disciples' response to him thus far must have been the greatest disappointment to Jesus. And yet now he is going to bring them to the point of realisation.

D. A double revelation for disciples (16:13-23)

1. – Peter's confession of Jesus (13-20)

Jesus brings the disciples to *Caesarea Philippi* (13a). This is an isolated region almost on Israel's northern border: it's as if Jesus is hanging a notice on the door saying *Please do not disturb*. He has been looking forward to this conversation.

When Jesus asks *Who do people say the Son of Man is?* (13b), he is simply asking who people think he is (see the parallel passage in Mark 8:27 for confirmation of this).

Section Four: The Son (Matthew 13:54 – 19:2) 101

After hearing the answers (see 14), Jesus asks the disciples the question everything has been leading up to: *But what about you? (…) Who do you say I am?* (15).

Peter replies on behalf of them all: he looks at Jesus and says *You are the Messiah, the Son of the living God* (16).

And heaven stands still.

This is the first time in Matthew's Gospel that someone has called Jesus *Messiah*: he is the saviour promised by God through the Old Testament prophets.

But Jesus is also, says Peter, *Son of the living God*, in a unique and special relationship with God (see chapter 14:33 and 3:17).

How must Jesus be feeling as he hears these words? We can guess the answer because of the joy which fills what he says: *Blessed are you, Simon son of Jonah, for this was not revealed to you by flesh and blood, but by my Father in heaven* (17).

So Peter has not reached his conclusion about Jesus' identity because of any special qualifications on his part, but because God has *revealed* this to him. We should notice, too, that by calling God *my Father in heaven*, Jesus is confirming his unique status as the Son.

Now Jesus has three further things to say to Peter.

First, he declares *I tell you that you are Peter, and on this rock I will build my church* (18a). Jesus had given him this new name much earlier (see Mark 3:16 and John 1:42); no one had ever been called Peter (*Kepa* in Aramaic) before this; and the name means *rock*.

So it is clear what Jesus means: Peter, already the leader of the disciple team (see chapter 10:2), will be the leader of the church, the messianic community, in its early years. This is something a quick read through of the first half of the book of Acts confirms.

But Jesus says nothing about Peter being infallible (he certainly wasn't!) or about his having a successor as leader.

And do you see how Jesus describes the church? It's *his*, and *the gates of Hades will not overcome it* (18b) – which is simply another way of saying that *it will never die*.

Second, Jesus tells Peter that he will give him *the keys of the kingdom of heaven* (19a), as the steward looking after it for his master.

Just before his ascension, Jesus will mention three people-groups to the disciples: Jews, Samaritans and Gentiles (see Acts 1:8). It is intriguing that Peter is the one who will open the door of the kingdom to these three groups (see Acts 2:36-41, 8:14-17 and 10:1-48).

Is this part of what Jesus means when he talks about giving Peter *the keys of the kingdom*?

And third, Jesus tells Peter that *whatever you bind on earth will be bound in heaven, and whatever you loose on earth will be loosed in heaven* (19). This is technical language for the forbidding or permitting of certain actions.

But this is not about Peter having authority to make decisions which God will rubber-stamp: literally the Greek reads that whatever he binds on earth *will have been bound* in heaven, and that whatever he looses on earth *will have been loosed* in heaven.

So in forbidding or permitting certain actions Peter will simply be passing on decisions *which have already been made* in heaven.

Matthew ends this extraordinary paragraph by letting us know that Jesus *ordered his disciples not to tell anyone that he was the Messiah* (20).

The reason is not hard to find. Popular expectation was that the Messiah would be a political king who would defeat the Romans so that Israel would be independent of any occupying power.

So the disciples are to tell no one that Jesus is the Messiah until they understand *what kind of Messiah* he is going to be.

This might be a good moment to read through verses 13-20 again. You might want to thank Jesus that you are part of the church, his messianic community, and to worship him that he is *the Messiah, the Son of the living God* (16).

2. – Jesus' first prediction (21-23)

Now Jesus begins to talk to his disciples about his suffering and death. This *has* to happen: *he must go to Jerusalem and suffer many things* (21a), and *he must be killed* (21b).

This necessity is there in Jesus' mind because he knows that this is the purpose of God the Father in sending him into the world.

This will all be *at the hands of the elders, the chief priests and the teachers of the law* (21): together these groups made up the Jewish ruling council. In other words, the tension between the religious leaders and Jesus is only going to get worse.

Section Four: The Son (Matthew 13:54 – 19:2)

Jesus also says that he will *on the third day be raised to life* (21b), but Peter probably hasn't heard this, so appalled is he by this talk of suffering and death: *Never, Lord! (…) This shall never happen to you!* (22) This doesn't fit with what Peter believes about the Messiah.

What Jesus says next must have come as a huge shock to Peter: *Get behind me, Satan! You are a stumbling-block to me* (23a). His best friend is calling him *Satan* the tempter.

And this must have been a real temptation to Jesus: it would be so much easier to be a political Messiah than a suffering one. So he tells Peter that his thinking is very human and not at all in line with God's view of things (see 23b).

The disciples have received two revelations about Jesus. First, he is the Messiah and the Son of God. And second, he will suffer and die.

And rise again.

E. Jesus: the disciples he wants (16:24 – 17:27)

Section Four's narrative part ends with another block of five incidents. All of them, in different ways, help us to understand what Jesus wants his disciples to look like.

1. – The call to discipleship (16:24-28)

Jesus talks here about what it costs to follow him: a person *must deny themselves* and *take up their cross* (24). Is this a hint about how he is going to die? He is certainly saying that all who follow a suffering Messiah must be willing to suffer themselves.

So Jesus spells out the result of deciding to live for ourselves: *Whoever wants to save their life will lose it* (25a). But for those who give their lives to serve Jesus and others there is good news: *Whover loses their life for me will find it* (25b).

Jesus goes on to explain that there is nothing more valuable than the human soul (see 26).

And now he reaches the climax of what he wants to say: *The Son of Man is going to come in his Father's glory with his angels* (27a). Jesus is again saying that he is the Son of God, and again saying that he is *the Son of Man*.

This time *Son of Man* is not just Jesus' way of talking about himself: there is much more here. He is saying that he is the glorious Son of Man depicted in Daniel 7:13 to whom all the nations will belong.

And he will judge them too: Jesus says he will *reward each person according to what they have done* (27b, see also chapter 25:31-46).

There is a surprise at the end of the paragraph. *Truly I tell you,* says Jesus, *some who are standing here will not taste death before they see the Son of Man coming in his kingdom* (28).

If Jesus is talking about his Second Coming in glory at the end of history, he was wrong. But, as we have already seen (see my comments on chapter 10:23), the coming of the Son of Man described in Daniel 7:13 is a coming *to* God, not a coming *from* God.

So Jesus is not referring here to his Second Coming but to his resurrection and exaltation.

And of that three of the disciples are about to get a preview.

2. – The transfiguration (17:1-13)

Jesus takes Peter, James and John up a mountain: *there he was transfigured before them. His face shone like the sun, and his clothes became as white as the light* (2).

They are seeing the glorious Son of Man (see chapter 16:28).

Moses and Elijah join Jesus (see 3): perhaps they represent the Old Testament revelation in the Law and the Prophets. This underlines the fact that Jesus is the one to whom the whole of history has been pointing (see my comments on chapter 1:1-17).

Peter is in danger of seeing no real distinction between Moses, Elijah and Jesus, as he suggests putting up shelters for all three (see 4).

But before he has finished his sentence a cloud appears and from it a voice says *This is my Son, whom I love; with him I am well pleased. Listen to him!* (5)

Matthew tells us about the three disciples' fear and Jesus' words *Don't be afraid* (7a), and adds that *when they looked up, they saw no one except Jesus* (8). The representatives of the Law and the Prophets give way to the one who fulfils both.

And that one is God's Son, declared authoritatively to be so by God the Father. He had said exactly the same words at Jesus' baptism (see chapter 3:17), but now he adds this command to the disciples: *Listen to him!* (5b)

If Peter, James and John are able to think clearly after what they have experienced on the mountain, this extra sentence will have reminded them of Moses' words about the Prophet-Messiah who would come one day (see Deut 18:15). In Jesus these words are being fulfilled.

But Jesus is more than a prophet and more than the Messiah: he is the *Son of God*, in a unique relationship with the Father. This has been an essential description of Jesus in this Gospel, and especially in Section Four's key incidents (see chapter 14:33; 16:16; 17:5).

On the way down the mountain the three disciples ask *Why then do the teachers of the law say that Elijah must come first?* (10)

Jesus replies that the theologians are correct (see Mal 3:1 and 4:5), but that *Elijah has already come* (12). He is referring to John the Baptist (see 13), who was not a reincarnation of Elijah (such an idea would contradict the Bible's teaching) but an Elijah-figure (see, for example, Luke 1:13-17 and my comments on chapter 11:14).

This is what Moses, Elijah and John the Baptist have in common: they prepared the way for Jesus, the Son of God.

And everyone who decides to follow Jesus must *listen to him* (5b).

3. – Jesus drives out an evil spirit (17:14-20)

A father asks Jesus to set his son free from a demon which tries to destroy him (see 14-15). He adds that *I brought him to your disciples, but they could not heal him* (16).

Jesus is disappointed by the nine disciples' lack of faith: he calls them an *unbelieving and perverse generation* (17a). When the boy is brought to him, he rebukes the demon. Matthew tells us that *it came out of the boy, and he was healed at that moment* (18).

Once again we see Jesus acting with effortless authority.

But the disciples who were not up the mountain with Jesus want to know why they have not been able to drive out the evil spirit (see 19): after all, he had given them authority to do such miracles (see chapter 10:1).

Jesus doesn't mince his words: it is *because you have so little faith* (20a). He goes on to say that *faith as small as a mustard seed* (20) will enable them to move mountains!

Faith is an indispensable characteristic of the disciples Jesus wants.

4. – Jesus' second prediction (17:22-23)

Now Jesus repeats to all twelve disciples what he has already told them: *The Son of Man is going to be delivered into the hands of men. They will kill him, and on the third day he will be raised to life* (22-23, see also chapter 16:21).

It looks like Matthew remembers the occasion and the effect it had on him and his friends. He tells us that *the disciples were filled with grief* (23b).

But, as we have already seen, disciples need to believe that this is why Jesus came.

5. – Paying the temple tax (17:24-27)

At the beginning of this incident, recounted only by Matthew, we learn that *the collectors of the two-drachma temple tax came to Peter* (24). They want to know if Jesus pays it or not.

Peter is confident of the answer: *Yes, he does* (25a).

Jesus, knowing about the conversation Peter has just had, asks him if kings collect tax from their own children or from other people (see 25b). Peter gives the obvious answer: *From others* (26a).

Then, says Jesus, *the children are exempt* (26b). He means that because the temple tax is God's tax, Jesus himself has no need to pay it. Jesus is not saying it in so many words, but here it is again: he is God's Son.

However, he decides to pay the tax anyway, *so that we may not cause offence* (27a). In the mouth of the first fish Peter catches he *will find a four-drachma coin. Take it and give it to them for my tax and yours* (27b).

Presumably this is exactly what happens: a miracle takes place which solves the temple tax problem, and at the same time shows that Jesus has a sense of humour!

As we arrive at the end of Section Four's narrative part it will do us good to look back for a few moments.

Despite the opposition from the religious leaders Jesus has continued to demonstrate his power as he transforms the lives of people in need.

And, all the while, he has been revealing his identity. The highpoint of Section Four is Peter's recognition that Jesus is *the Messiah, the Son of the living God* (see chapter 16:16).

One reason Matthew wrote his Gospel is to help us to come to the same conclusion.

Teaching (18:1-35)

Section Four's teaching part is about relationships in the Jesus community, which is now called the church (see 17, and chapter 16:18).

Jesus clearly expects that those who follow him will have a sense of belonging to one another.

How does he want disciples to behave in their relationships together?

A. Be small (18:1-5)

The disciples ask Jesus the big question: *Who, then, is the greatest in the kingdom of heaven?* (1) To help him answer the question, Jesus calls a little child (see 2).

1. – Becoming like a little child (2-4)

People who want to enter God's kingdom, says Jesus, need to *become like little children* (3). And then he explains what he means: *Whoever takes the lowly position of this child is the greatest in the kingdom of heaven* (4).

In Jewish society a child was viewed as unimportant, so this is about our making a decision: I am not going to big myself up by impressing others, but instead be willing to be seen as insignificant.

The church is a community, not a competition. It is fine to want to be the greatest, provided we undertand how that can be achieved.

2. – Welcoming a little child (5)

Disciples of Jesus are not to treat little children the way wider society does. Jesus shows how *he* sees children by explaining that *whoever welcomes one such child in my name welcomes me* (5).

Something interesting is going on here. When he talks about *one such child,* Jesus is not only talking about children but also about disciples who have accepted the status of a child (see 3).

Jesus will now start to talk about *little ones* (6,10,14), as a way of talking about disciples who might seem insignificant (see also chapter 10:42 and 11:25).

B. Be careful (18:6-9)

Now Jesus addresses the danger of causing people to stumble: we are to be careful about how we behave.

1. – Causing others to stumble (6-7)

If someone trips up another disciple (*one of these little ones,* 6a) in some way, Jesus takes that incredibly seriously: *it would be better for them to have a large millstone hung round their neck and to be drowned in the depths of the sea* (6b).

I might cause you to stumble by not listening to you, or by obviously not respecting you.

Jesus uses strong language to jerk us into action: such things will happen, but *woe to the person through whom they come!* (7b)

2. – Causing myself to stumble (8-9)

Jesus says we need to take sin seriously: if we don't we are playing with fire (see 8b, 9b; see also my comments on chapter 5:29-30).

His comments about cutting off a hand or a foot and gouging out an eye (see 8 and 9) are deliberate exaggeration to emphasize the need for radical action against sin in our lives. The hand may refer to something I do, the foot to somewhere I go, and the eye to something I look at.

Jesus is warning that it is a dangerous thing to take sin lightly. If I make a habit of falling into this trap and causing myself to stumble, how do I know that I am really a disciple of Jesus?

C. Be caring (18:10-14)

Jesus is still referring to disciples as *little ones* (10, 14): all of us are vulnerable and need care from others.

1. – Respecting little ones (10)

Those who follow Jesus should *not despise one of these little ones* (10a). Some people have no contact with others who respect them, but that should not be the case in the church.

And Jesus gives an intriguing reason for this: *their angels in heaven always see the face of my Father in heaven* (10b).

Jesus is saying that everyone in the disciple community has an angel representing them in heaven, which means that everyone has personal access to God.

How can I *not* respect someone who is in personal relationship with the Creator?

2. – Rescuing little ones (11-14)

Jesus tells the parable of the lost sheep in Luke's Gospel: there the lost sheep is a person who has not yet come to trust him (see Luke 15:3-7).

Section Four: The Son (Matthew 13:54 – 19:2)   109

Here, however, the lost sheep is someone who is already part of the Jesus community, but who has wandered off for some reason.

So what will a shepherd do who owns a hundred sheep but *one of them wanders away* (12a)? He will *leave the ninety-nine on the hills and go to look for the one that wandered off* (12b).

In the same way, says Jesus, *your Father in heaven is not willing that any of these little ones should perish* (14).

The lesson seems to be that because of this we should be willing to try to rescue someone who has wandered off.

If they matter to us, that is what we will do.

D. Be discreet (18:15-20)

This paragraph is about helping other disciples who are caught up in a sin in some way. Of course we are not to *judge* one another (see chapter 7:1); but we are to give one another a helping hand.

1. – Step One (15)

If your brother or sister sins, says Jesus, *go and point out their fault* (15a). But this should be done in private: *just between the two of you* (15a).

Among other things this is designed to prevent gossip: we are to be discreet.

And the aim is to help: *If they listen to you, you have won them over* (15b).

But of course that will not always work.

2. – Step Two (16)

Jesus tells us what to do *if they will not listen* (16a). I am to *take one or two others along* (16a), presumably to encourage my friend to take the issue seriously.

Once again, the watchword is *discretion*.

And Jesus backs up this course of action with a quotation from the Old Testament. I take one or two others along with me so that *every matter may be established by the testimony of two or three witnesses* (16b, quoting Deut 19:15).

3. – Step Three (17-20)

And what am I to do *if they still refuse to listen* (17a)? I should *tell it to the church* (17a), to the local community of disciples.

And, says Jesus, *if they refuse to listen even to the church, treat them as you would a pagan or a tax collector* (17b).

This is not primarily about what we would call church discipline, but rather about the power of persuasion. If everyone gives this person the cold shoulder it may well prompt them to think again and to repent of their sin.

The end of verse 17 doesn't mean that Jesus agrees with the idea of keeping Gentiles and tax collectors at arm's length: we know this because we have already seen Jesus loving such people (see chapter 8:5-13 and 9:9-13).

Jesus is simply using a proverbial expression to explain what course of action to take if a disciple committing a sin sets themselves against the united judgment of the community.

And now Jesus says something he has already said to Peter. But now he is talking to the church (the word *you* is plural here): *Whatever you bind on earth will be bound in heaven, and whatever you loose on earth will be loosed in heaven* (18, see also chapter 16:19).

This is picture language to explain that the Jesus community has the authority to call some behaviour sin (*binding on earth*) and other behaviour fully acceptable (*loosing on earth*).

But it's not the *church* making the decision: the Greek says literally that what the church binds on earth *will have been bound* in heaven. In other words, it is God who makes such a decision, and the church – on the basis of what God has revealed in Scripture – passes it on.

The paragraph ends with Jesus encouraging his disciples to pray. If two people are bringing a request to God *it will be done for them* (19b).

But there are two conditions.

First, they need to *agree about anything they ask for* (19a). And second, says Jesus, they need to be meeting *in my name* (20), wanting to do his will and to bring him glory.

And whenever two disciples meet up with that in mind, they can be sure of something: *there am I with them* (20).

This is an extraordinary promise. He may not be present physically, but he will be *with them*. And this is Jesus, the one who can talk about *my Father in heaven* (19b).

This is the Son of God (see also chapter 14:33; 16:16).

E. Be forgiving (18:21-35)

Disciples of Jesus are still sinners, so they need to be ready to repent and forgive. This is the issue Peter has in mind here.

1. – Peter's question (21-22)

Lord, how many times shall I forgive my brother or sister who sins against me? (21) The rabbis of the time reckoned that three times was the maximum.

So Peter's suggestion is generous: *Up to seven times?* (21b)

Jesus, in reply, tells him that he should forgive *seventy-seven times* (22). The footnote in NIV2011 suggests that this could be *seventy times seven*, but if we are concerned as to whether the figure is 77 or 490, we really have missed the point!

And Jesus makes that point now.

2. – Jesus' parable (23-34)

The story is about a servant who is forgiven a huge debt by his master, the king: *The servant's master took pity on him, cancelled the debt and let him go* (27).

And this debt is *huge*: as the highest Greek numeral is *ten thousand*, we might well say that the servant owed *a billion pounds*.

When Jesus says that the man's master *took pity* on him (27), he uses the words Matthew used in referring to what Jesus felt when seeing the crowds in Section Two of the Gospel: *compassion* (see chapter 9:36).

But then the servant refuses to forgive the debt of a man who owes him *a hundred silver coins* (28). This is ludicrous behaviour: this second debt is one six-hundred-thousandth of the first!

The master sends for him and calls him a *wicked servant* (32a). He goes on: *I cancelled all that debt of yours because you begged me to. Shouldn't you have had mercy on your fellow servant just as I had on you?* (32b-33)

So we reach the climax of the story: *In anger his master handed him over to the jailers to be tortured, until he should pay back all he owed* (34).

3. – Our responsibility (35)

Jesus' explanation of the parable is swift and to the point: *This is how my heavenly Father will treat each of you unless you forgive your brother or sister from your heart* (35).

Jesus has already made this clear when teaching about prayer in Section One (see chapter 6:12, 14-15).

But there is more.

Those who have started to follow Jesus have been forgiven their huge debt of sin: is there a hint here that Jesus will go to the cross to make that possible?

But, forgiven ourselves, we have a responsibility to forgive others. The church is the community of the forgiven: our task is to live that out in practice.

Now Matthew signals that we have reached the end of Section Four. *When Jesus had finished saying these things,* he says, *he left Galilee and went into the region of Judea to the other side of the Jordan* (chapter 19:1, compare 7:28; 11:1; 13:53).

But the geographical change of scene doesn't change things: Jesus continues to reach out to people, as *large crowds followed him, and he healed them there* (2).

Learning the Gospel

I hope you will take the time to learn the order of the events in Section Four: it is not difficult and it is absolutely worthwhile.

Begin with the narrative part. Learn the five headings in bold: remember that saying them out loud will make this much easier.

Now concentrate on the five incidents in block A. Repeat them a few times and you will soon get them lodged in your mind.

Block B will be easy to learn, because there are only two warnings here to get your head around.

Now do the same with the five incidents in block C, and then with blocks D and E.

As you commit these incidents to memory, you will find that all kinds of details occur to you.

After you have learnt the narrative part of the section, the teaching part will seem very easy: it is short and to the point. First learn the five headings in bold; then learn the sub-headings.

Section Four: The Son Narrative

A. Jesus: the authority he demonstrates
1. Opposition in Nazareth
2. The death of John the Baptist
3. The feeding of the 5,000
4. Jesus walks on the water
5. Healings in Gennesaret

B. A double warning for disciples
1. God's word and human tradition
2. What makes people unclean?

C. Jesus: the responses he gets
1. Jesus and the Canaanite woman
2. Jesus heals many Gentiles
3. Feeding of the 4,000
4. The Pharisees and the Sadducees demand a sign
5. The confusion of the disciples

D. A double revelation for disciples
1. Peter's confession of Jesus
2. Jesus' first prediction

E. Jesus: the disciples he wants
1. The call to discipleship
2. The transfiguration
3. Jesus drives out an evil spirit
4. Jesus' second prediction
5. Paying the temple tax

Teaching

A. Be small
1. Becoming like a little child
2. Welcoming a little child

B. Be careful
1. Causing others to stumble
2. Causing myself to stumble

C. Be caring
1. Respecting little ones
2. Rescuing little ones

D. Be discreet
1. Step One
2. Step Two
3. Step Three

E. Be forgiving
1. Peter's question
2. Jesus' parable
3. Our responsibility

'When Jesus had finished...'

Meeting the Lord

The purpose of Matthew's Gospel is not only that we get information about Jesus, but also that we get to know him better.

Running through the titles of the incidents, add any details which occur to you. As you do so, talk to the Lord about what you are remembering: you will be meeting Jesus.

And remember that you could do this on your own, or with a friend who has also learnt Section Four.

In the narrative part's incidents, thank him for his power and love as he reveals his identity. And when you run through the teaching part in your mind, ask Jesus to help you to put what he says into action.

This is the Matthew experiment: as you re-tell Matthew, you will rediscover Jesus.

Section Five: The Judge
Matthew 19:3 – 26:2

We have already seen in this Gospel that Jesus has the authority to judge because he is in a unique relationship with God the Father. Now, in Section Five, we will watch Jesus as he makes judgments on many issues, pronounces judgment on the leaders of Israel and proclaims his return as Judge at the end of history. And, in the centre of the section, we will see him arrive in Jerusalem as king.

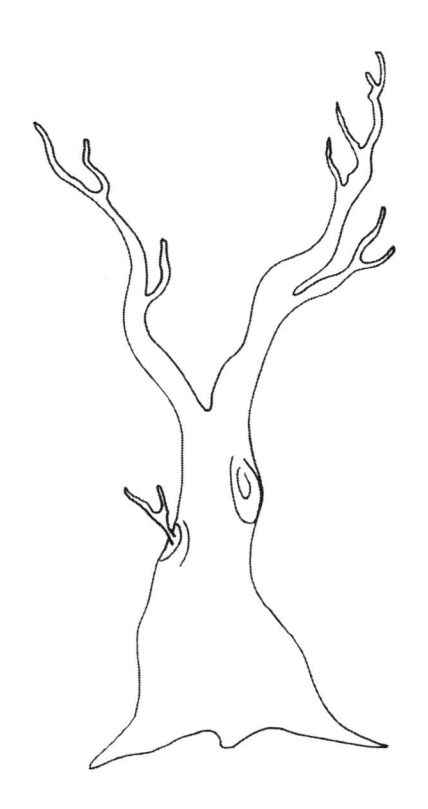

> Seeing a fig-tree by the road, he went up to it
> but found nothing on it except leaves.
> Then he said to it,
> 'May you never bear fruit again!'
> Immediately the tree withered.
>
> Matthew 21:19

Enjoying the View

Narrative (19:3 – 22:46)

A. Three issues Jesus addresses (19:3-26)
1. Marriage (3-12)
2. Children (13-15)
3. Possessions (16-26)

B. Three rewards Jesus promises (19:27 – 20:16)
1. Disciples will share his victory (19:28)
2. Disciples will gain more than they give up (19:29)
3. Disciples will experience the surprises of the new age (19:30 – 20:16)

C. Three things Jesus does *before* entering Jerusalem (20:17-34)
1. Jesus' third prediction (17-19)
2. The Zebedee family request (20-28)
3. The healing of two blind men (29-34)

D. Jesus enters Jerusalem (21:1-11)
1. What Jesus does (1-7)
2. What the crowds shout (8-9)
3. What everyone asks (10-11)

E. Three things Jesus does *after* entering Jerusalem (21:12-27)
1. He clears the temple (12-17)
2. He curses the fig-tree (18-22)
3. He confuses the religious leaders (23-27)

F. Three parables Jesus tells (21:28 – 22:14)
1. The two sons (28-32)
2. The tenants (33-46)
3. The wedding banquet (22:1-14)

G. Three traps Jesus avoids (22:15-46)
1. Paying taxes to Caesar (15-22)

Section Five: The Judge (Matthew 19:3 – 26:2)

   2. Marriage at the resurrection (23-33)
   3. The greatest commandment (34-40)

Teaching (23:1 – 26:2)

A. Judgment on the scribes and the Pharisees (23:1-39)
   1. Warning about the scribes and the Pharisees (1-12)
   2. Condemnation of the scribes and the Pharisees (13-36)
   3. Bad news for the scribes and the Pharisees (37-39)

B. Judgment in the fall of Jerusalem (24:1-35)
   1. The end is not yet (4-8)
   2. How to live in the meantime (9-14)
   3. How to recognise the Judean crisis (15-28)
   4. The temple's destruction and the Son's triumph (29-31)
   5. Jesus' answer to the disciples' first question (32-35)

C. Judgment at the return of Jesus (24:36 – 25:46)
   1. His coming: unpredictable and inescapable (24:36-41)
   2. Our readiness (24:42 – 25:30)
      a. the parable of the servant put in charge (24:45-51)
      b. the parable of the girls waiting for the bridegroom (25:1-13)
      c. the parable of the servants given lots of money (25:14-30)
   3. His judgment: final and authoritative (25:31-46)

'When Jesus had finished…' (26:1-2)

The narrative part of Section Five is structured around a series of blocks of three incidents, with Jesus' entry into Jerusalem on a donkey as the centrepiece.

The teaching part here is long: Jesus warns of judgment in the present, in the impending fall of Jerusalem and at his return in glory at the end of human history.

Before reading further in this book, please read the whole section in Matthew's. Imagine the reactions of people as they hear Jesus, and talk to him yourself about what you are reading.

This is an essential part of the Matthew experiment.

Unpacking the Content

Narrative (19:3 – 22:46)

A. Three issues Jesus addresses (19:3-26)

At the end of Section Four Matthew has told us that Jesus has come *into the region of Judea* (see chapter 19:1). So he is deliberately moving towards Jerusalem and to the climax of his story.

1. – Marriage (3-12)

Jesus takes the opportunity to address this issue when the Pharisees turn up with a question about divorce: *Is it lawful for a man to divorce his wife for any and every reason?* (3)

Jesus returns to the creation account in the book of Genesis. Because God made man and woman, *for this reason a man will leave his father and mother and be united to his wife, and the two will become one flesh* (5, quoting Gen 2:24).

Jesus concludes *Therefore what God has joined together, let no one separate* (6b).

But the Pharisees are not finished yet: *Why then (…) did Moses command that a man give his wife a certificate of divorce and send her away?* (7)

Jesus notices that they use the word *command* and corrects their mistake by replying that *Moses permitted you to divorce your wives* (8a): he makes it clear that this was not God's original purpose but *because your hearts were hard* (8).

The implication of verse 9 is that divorce ought only to be contemplated where adultery has taken place: otherwise the marriage is not over and any *remarriage* is itself adultery.

So Jesus is saying that divorce is always an evil. But sometimes it may be a *lesser* evil.

It is no wonder that the disciples' reaction to this is to suggest that *it is better not to marry* (10).

Jesus' reply (see 11-12) is not recommending celibacy, as he has already made clear that marriage is God's good creation purpose for humanity (see 4-5).

What he is saying is that some people are *called* to celibacy: they are people *to whom it has been given* (11).

Section Five: The Judge (Matthew 19:3 – 26:2) 119

One more thing is worth adding here before we move on. Back in verses 4 and 5 Jesus quotes from the second chapter of Genesis. He says that *the Creator (...) said 'For this reason a man will leave his father and mother...'*

But in the Genesis account those words are not the words of God but the words of the writer. This is not a slip on Jesus' part: this just makes it very clear that, for Jesus, *what Scripture says, God says.*

2. – Children (13-15)

The disciples are not happy that people bring small children to Jesus and ask him for prayer: they *rebuked them* (13).

But Jesus tells the disciples to let the children through and tells them why: *the kingdom of heaven belongs to such as these* (14b). Children, seen as insignificant in first-century Jewish culture (see my comments on chapter 18:1-5), will be welcomed into God's kingdom.

We should not forget here that the phrase *such as these* (14) refers not only to children but to all who have started to follow Jesus and who may be seen as unimportant by others.

3. – Possessions (16-26)

A young man (see 20, 22) asks Jesus *What good thing must I do to get eternal life?* (16)

Jesus wants to show him that while the ambition (*eternal life*) is great, his understanding about how to get there (*What good thing must I do..?*) is wrong.

So he tells the young man that *there is only One who is good* (17). Because God is absolutely good, no human being can hope to reach him by doing a deed *they* think of as good.

Jesus takes him back to basics by saying *If you want to enter life, keep the commandments* (17b). Then he lists five which are all concerned with right relationships with other people: this is confirmed by his adding *Love your neighbour as yourself* (18-19, quoting Exod 20:12-16 and Lev 19:18).

The young man's answer shows that he thinks righteousness is just about keeping the rules: he tells Jesus *All these I have kept* (20a). He clearly thinks that this is a test he is going to pass easily.

Asked what else the young man needs to do, Jesus tells him to *sell your possessions and give to the poor* (21a). This is a test the man has not reckoned with. The question is: does he love God more than his wealth?

And Jesus is promising him *real* wealth if he puts God first: if he does all this he *will have treasure in heaven* and can follow Jesus (21b, see also chapter 6:20-21).

Matthew tells us what happens next: *When the young man heard this, he went away sad, because he had great wealth* (22).

And Jesus watches him go.

Now the disciples are going to learn the lesson: it is hard for rich people, says Jesus, to enter God's kingdom. To make the point clearer still, he adds that *it is easier for a camel to go through the eye of a needle than for someone who is rich to enter the kingdom of God* (24).

In other words: humanly speaking, it is impossible.

The disciples are *greatly astonished* at this (25), because they assume that wealth and possessions are more or less a guarantee that someone is already accepted by God.

When they ask *Who then can be saved?* (25b), Jesus replies *With man this is impossible, but with God all things are possible* (26).

There is nothing wrong with possessions: we all have them. But this incident urges us to ask ourselves what is more important to us: what we have or following Jesus.

We have heard Jesus giving his judgment about three crucial issues. Now Peter (and presumably the other disciples, too) wants to know about rewards.

B. Three rewards Jesus promises (19:27 – 20:16)

Peter is wondering what he and the other disciples are going to get out of being in the Jesus team: *We have left everything to follow you! What then will there be for us?* (27)

Jesus replies that they will have three rewards.

1. – Disciples will share his victory (28)

Jesus is talking about *the renewal of all things* (28). Literally the word is *rebirth*, which is the time when heaven and earth are made new.

Jesus, *the Son of Man,* will be victorious because he will sit *on his glorious throne* (28, see also Dan 7:13-14).

Now comes the breathtaking reward: *You who have followed me will also sit on twelve thrones, judging the twelve tribes of Israel* (28).

They will share Jesus' victory.

Section Five: The Judge (Matthew 19:3 – 26:2) 121

2. – Disciples will gain more than they give up (29)

People who make the decision to follow Jesus may have some *leaving* to do (*houses, brothers, sisters, father, mother, wife, children, fields*): if they do, says Jesus, they are doing it *for my sake* (29).

So discipleship may involve some losses.

But the gains are infinitely greater. Disciples *will receive a hundred times as much* – presumably in this life – *and will inherit eternal life* in the next.

The gains now are to be found in the church, the Jesus community; the gains in the future will be enjoyed *at the renewal of all things* (28a).

So no one who gives up some things in order to follow Jesus will end up losing out.

3. – Disciples will experience the surprises of the new age (19:30 – 20:16)

Matthew has written this whole paragraph as one unit: comparing chapter 19:30 with chapter 20:16 makes that clear. The bookends either side of this parable show that Jesus' teaching turns the world's values upside down.

The story is about *a landowner who went out early in the morning to hire workers for his vineyard* (1). Jesus adds that *he agreed to pay them a denarius for the day* (2), which is the usual daily wage.

There are two surprises about the landowner.

First, he keeps inviting more workers into his vineyard. He goes out to the market-place again at 9am, 12noon, 3pm and 5pm and says to those he finds *You also go and work in my vineyard* (4a, 7b, see also 3, 5, 6).

And, *second,* he is unbelievably generous. Instead of giving those who started work much later a small proportion of a denarius, he gives every worker the full wage: *each received a denarius* (9b).

This is true of those who have worked all day long, too: the result is that they *grumble against the landowner* (11).

But his response is firm: *Don't I have the right to do what I want with my own money? Or are you envious because I am generous?* (15)

This parable is not intended to provide us with a pattern for labour relations! Jesus tells it in order to let disciples know that there will be surprises in the new age.

First, we will find that God has called people to follow him at different times in their lives. Some will have become disciples as children, and others as pensioners.

And, *second,* we will find that God is unbelievably generous. If I complain about people who became disciples shortly before their death being rewarded as much as me, then I have not understood what *grace* is: deep down I believe that I have *earned* something from God.

Jesus is telling us to be ready to be surprised: *The last will be first, and the first will be last* (chapter 20:16, see also 19:30).

Of the three rewards Jesus promises disciples, this third one is probably the most challenging. But all three provide a powerful motivation to be a passionate disciple of Jesus.

C. Three things Jesus does *before* entering Jerusalem (20:17-34)

1. – Jesus' third prediction (17-19)

Since the beginning of Section Five Jesus has been in Judea (see chapter 19:1); now Matthew tells us that he is *going up to Jerusalem* (17a).

But Jesus says it to the disciples too: *We are going up to Jerusalem* (18a). The tension is increasing: the ultimate drama is about to begin.

This prediction is more detailed than the others regarding what will happen to *the Son of Man* (18, and compare chapter 16:21 and 17:22-23). *The chief priests and the teachers of the law* will *condemn him to death* (18b): the representatives of the nation are going to reject Jesus.

These religious leaders, says Jesus, *will hand him over to the Gentiles* (19a). And he leaves the disciples in no doubt as to what the Gentiles will do: he will *be mocked and flogged and crucified* (19a).

This is the first time Jesus has specified *how* he will be killed. His death will be the most degrading and humiliating of all: he will die on a cross.

Matthew doesn't tell us how the disciples react to this renewed prediction of Jesus' suffering. And we don't know if they register the last thing Jesus says about the Son of Man: *On the third day he will be raised to life!* (19b)

2. – The Zebedee family request (20-28)

Jesus is asked a favour: *Then the mother of Zebedee's sons came to Jesus* (20). She is part of the disciple group on the move with Jesus (see chapter 27:56) and is ambitious for James and John.

She may know already that the disciples will all sit on thrones in the new age (see chapter 19:28); but now she asks Jesus to *grant that one of these two sons of mine may sit at your right and the other at your left in your kingdom* (21b).

Jesus tells the mother *You don't know what you are asking* (22a) and asks the sons *Can you drink the cup I am going to drink?* (22b) They are confident that they can: perhaps they don't see the cup as an Old Testament metaphor for imminent suffering (see, for example, Isa 51:17; Jer 25:17ff).

Jesus assures James and John that they *will* drink the cup of suffering, but adds that *he* is not the one who allots the places in his kingdom (see 23).

When the ten other disciples get wind of the Zebedee family request, *they were indignant with the two brothers* (24), probably because James and John have got in first.

So Jesus calls them all together. He describes how Gentile rulers exert their authority and says *Not so with you* (26a).

Then he explains that true greatness means a servant lifestyle, for *whoever wants to become great among you must be your servant* (26).

And now Jesus tells the disciples two things about himself.

First, he is their example: *the Son of Man did not come to be served, but to serve* (28a). If Jesus lived this way, so should we.

And, *second*, he is their ransom: he came *to give his life as a ransom for many* (28b). We all know what a ransom is: it's a price paid to set others free.

Jesus is saying that what he does on the cross will be *voluntary* (he will *give* his life) and *substitutionary*: his death will pay the price for our sins (see Isa 52:13 – 53:12 for the background).

This is the clearest statement in Matthew's Gospel of the meaning of Jesus' death.

3. – The healing of two blind men (29-34)

We know from Mark's Gospel that one of these two blind men is called Bartimaeus (see Mk 10:46-52). They clearly know enough about Jesus to want to ask for help from the *Son of David* (30b): he is the Jewish Messiah.

Despite the crowd telling them to be quiet they keep shouting *Lord, Son of David, have mercy on us!* (31)

What Matthew writes next is extraordinary: *Jesus stopped* (32a).

Despite his focus on his suffering and death, Jesus is still committed to service: when the two men tell him *We want our sight* (33), we read that *Jesus had compassion on them* (34a, see also chapter 9:36).

So he touches their eyes. Then Matthew tells us that *immediately they received their sight and followed him* (34b).

D. Jesus enters Jerusalem (21:1-11)

The writers of all four Gospels report this key event, but Matthew puts the emphasis on three things in particular which point to the identity of Jesus.

1. – What Jesus does (1-7)

Throughout his ministry Jesus normally walked everywhere; now, for the only time, he is riding on a donkey. He has made careful preparations for this (see 1-3).

This is an important moment for Matthew, because it is time for another of his fulfilment quotations: *This took place to fulfil what was spoken through the prophet* (4, see also my comments on chapter 8:17a).

So Matthew quotes *Say to your daughter Zion, 'See, your king comes to you, gentle and riding on a donkey, and on a colt, the foal of a donkey'* (5, quoting Zech 9:9).

This was recognised as referring to the Messiah. And now Jesus comes, deliberately fulfilling this prophecy: it is as if he is arriving in Jerusalem holding a huge placard with the words on it *I am the Messiah!*

2. – What the crowds shout (8-9)

When they call out *Blessed is he who comes in the name of the Lord!* they are quoting the climax of the Hallel Psalms (113-118), which were chanted at all the great festivals of Israel (see Ps 118:25-26).

But they add something.

They are shouting their hosannas *to the Son of David!* (9) It looks like many people are thinking that Jesus could be the fulfilment of messianic expectation.

3. – What everyone asks (10-11)

Of the four Gospel-writers, only Matthew tells us that *when Jesus entered Jerusalem, the whole city was stirred and asked 'Who is this?'* (10)

Many people are saying that he is *the prophet from Nazareth in Galilee* (11). Do they mean that he is just *a* prophet, or do they mean that he is *the* Prophet-Messiah promised through Moses (see Deut 18:15-18)?

Matthew doesn't say. But surely he tells us the question *the whole city* (10) was asking, because he wants us, his readers, to be asking that question too.

Who is this man?

E. Three things Jesus does *after* entering Jerusalem (21:12-27)

1. – He clears the temple (12-17)

Jesus walks into the headquarters of first-century Jewish religion as if he owns the place (which he does).

He drives out people from the market stalls and overturns the tables and benches of the money-changers and the dove-sellers (see 12).

To explain his actions Jesus quotes God's words in the prophecy of Isaiah: *My house will be called a house of prayer* (13, quoting: Isa 56:7). But now, he says, it is *a den of robbers* (13b, quoting Jer 7:11).

The people of God are supposed to be in relationship with God: talking to him should be central. But the temple seems to be anything but *a house of prayer.*

When *the chief priests and the teachers of the law* (15a) see the miracles Jesus is doing (see 14) and hear children shouting out that Jesus is *the Son of David* (15b), Matthew tells us that *they were indignant* (15b).

And when the chief priests and the scribes expect him to correct the children, Jesus replies that this is simply fulfilling what Scripture says: *From the lips of children and infants you, Lord, have called forth your praise* (16b, quoting Ps 8:2).

By clearing the temple Jesus has provoked the leaders of Israel.

2. – He curses the fig-tree (18-22)

When Jesus is hungry and sees a fig-tree, *he went up to it but found nothing on it except leaves* (19).

The fig-tree is an Old Testament picture for the nation of Israel (see, for example, Micah 7:1). So when Jesus curses the tree and it withers, this is a visual message of judgment: in cursing the fig-tree Jesus is explaining what he did in the temple the day before.

It's like he's saying to the religious leaders *Your religion is all leaves and no fruit.*

And now Jesus teaches the disciples about the fruit that was missing in the temple: prayer (see 13).

And the emphasis is on the importance of trusting God. Prayer will be answered *if you have faith and do not doubt* (21a) and *if you believe* (22).

It's like Jesus is saying to the disciples *Don't let the same thing be true of you that is true of temple religion.*

3. – He confuses the religious leaders (23-27)

Back in the temple, Jesus is approached by *the chief priests and the elders of the people* (23a). They ask him *By what authority are you doing these things? (23b)*

Jesus replies that he will answer their question if they will answer his: *John's baptism – where did it come from?* (25a)

This is not a random question, because John the Baptist's baptism pointed forward to Jesus' own arrival on the scene. Saying that John's baptism was from God would mean acknowledging that Jesus' authority was from God, too.

So the religious leaders are in a quandary: if they say John's baptism was *from heaven,* Jesus will tell them their unbelief is not logical (see 25b).

But they can't say it was *of human origin (26a),* because, as they say to each other, *we are afraid of the people, for they all hold that John was a prophet* (26).

So they are confused as to what to say. There is only one option open to them: *We don't know* (27a).

And now, having been attacked by the religious leaders, Jesus moves on to the attack himself.

F. Three parables Jesus tells (21:28 – 22:14)

The order in which Jesus tells these is not arbitrary.

When Jesus explains the first parable, he focuses on people's response to the preaching of John the Baptist (see 32); while the servants in the second parable are the Old Testament prophets, the climax of the story is the rejection of the Son (see 37-39); the servants in the third parable are the apostles and the early church as they invite people to the king's wedding banquet for his son (see chapter 22:2-3).

So you could say that the three parables provide us with an overview of church history.

1. – The two sons (28-32)

The story is simple. A father wants to send his sons to work in his vineyard.

One son says *No,* but then goes. The other says *Yes,* but doesn't go. So, says Jesus to *the chief priests and the elders of the people* (23a), *which of the two did what his father wanted?* (31a)

In other words: what matters is not what you say but what you do.

This is why *the tax collectors and the prostitutes are entering the kingdom of God ahead of you* (31b). For when John the Baptist came to preach, *you did not believe him, but the tax collectors and the prostitutes did* (32a).

And even the shock of seeing such sinners turn to God had no effect on the religious leaders: *Even after you saw this, you did not repent and believe* John the Baptist (32b).

2. – The tenants (33-46)

The vineyard, which we have already met in the first parable (see 28), is another Old Testament picture for the nation of Israel: Jesus' description in verse 33 is practically lifted from the prophecy of Isaiah (see Isa 5:2).

The *landowner who planted a vineyard* and who then rents it out to tenants (see 33) is God; the tenants are the leaders of Israel. The servants he sends to the tenants at harvest time are the prophets.

It's interesting *why* he sends them: it's *to collect his fruit* (34).

But instead of finding the qualities God expects to characterise his people, his prophets were mistreated: *they beat one, killed another and stoned a third* (35).

So Jesus tells us what the landowner does: *Last of all, he sent his son to them* because he thought *They will respect my son* (37).

But when the tenants see the son they say to each other *This is the heir. Come, let's kill him and take his inheritance* (38). There is something important to notice here: their argument only makes sense if the landowner has died.

Whether Jesus' listeners get this or not, it's like Jesus is saying to them: *You're behaving as if God were dead.*

So what do the tenants do to the landowner's son? *They took him and threw him out of the vineyard and killed him* (39).

Imagine how Jesus is feeling as he says those words! He knows that this is about him: the landowner's son is the Son of God, who will soon be done away with by the leaders of Israel.

When Jesus asks his listeners what they would expect the vineyard owner to do, they reply that he will kill the tenants (see 41a) and *rent the vineyard to other tenants, who will give him his share of the crop at harvest time* (41b).

They've understood the story, but not yet understood its meaning.

So Jesus does two things.

First, he quotes from the Old Testament again: *the stone the builders rejected has become the cornerstone* (42, quoting Ps 118:22-23). The picture is different now, but the message is the same: Jesus is the stone rejected by the religious leader-builders, which will bring judgment on them (see 44).

And second, he stops using pictures altogether. In a statement found only in Matthew's Gospel, Jesus tells Israel's leaders that *the kingdom of God will be taken away from you and given to a people who will produce its fruit* (43).

The message is clear: there is to be a new people of God in place of Old Testament Israel. This new people is the church, made up of Jews *and* Gentiles who trust in Jesus the Son.

Of course this *doesn't* mean that God has stopped loving the Jewish nation. But it *does* mean that the people of God is now the church.

Matthew tells us that *the chief priests and the Pharisees (...) knew he was talking about them* (45). Now, at last, they do get it.

But, instead of repenting, *they looked for a way to arrest him* (46a).

3. – The wedding banquet (22:1-14)

The third parable is about *a king who prepared a wedding banquet for his son* (2). He sends his servants to those who have been invited, *but they refused to come* (3).

Despite the meal being ready (see 4), *they paid no attention and went off – one to his field, another to his business* (5).

But there is worse to come: *the rest seized his servants, ill-treated them and killed them* (6).

Now Jesus tells us that the king is angry (see 7a): *he sent his army and destroyed those murderers and burned their city* (7b).

That last phrase is a clue to the meaning of the story.

It looks like Jesus is talking about the destruction of Jerusalem (or at least of the temple) in AD 70: this will happen as a result of Israel's refusal to respond to God's invitation through the Jesus community.

We have already met the idea of a new people of God at the conclusion of the first two parables (see chapter 21:31-32, 41-43); now, here it is again at the conclusion of the third.

The king tells his servants to *go to the street corners and invite to the banquet anyone you find* (9), with the result that *the wedding hall was filled with guests* (10b).

This is the new people of God, made up of Jews *and* Gentiles who accept God's invitation through the church.

But Jesus adds something: one of the guests is *not wearing wedding clothes* (11b).

In the context of the three parables, and indeed of everything we have learnt since Jesus has arrived in Jerusalem, the *wedding clothes* are a reference to a life which shows the fruit which belongs to the people of God (see, for example, chapter 21:13, 19, 41b, 43b).

If someone's life is not changed by having been invited to God's celebration, that shows that they don't really belong to God's people at all.

And the consequences are serious, as Jesus makes clear (see 13).

The parable ends with an epigram: *Many are invited, but few are chosen* (14). The church is going to invite many people to accept the divine invitation, but there are going to be many whose response reveals that God has never been at work in their lives at all.

So Jesus has told his three parables. They contain two very important lessons.

First, because of Israel's rejection of Jesus, the church is the new people of God, made up of Jews and Gentiles who respond to God's invitation.

And, *second*, God expects his people to have fruit in their lives which shows that they really belong to him.

G. Three traps Jesus avoids (22:15-46)

After what they have just heard, the religious leaders are feeling even more hostile towards Jesus. So they come up with some trick questions.

1. – Paying taxes to Caesar (15-22)

The Pharisees would normally have nothing in common with the Herodians, who are a political group sympathetic to the Romans (see 15-16a).

But now they have found common cause.

After a display of heavy-handed flattery (see 16b), they ask Jesus *Is it right to pay the poll-tax to Caesar or not?* (17)

But Jesus is not fooled. He calls them *hypocrites* (see also chapter 15:7) and asks *Why are you trying to trap me?* (18)

His questioners acknowledge that the image of Caesar is on the denarius coin, so Jesus says *Give back to Caesar what is Caesar's, and to God what is God's* (21).

Obviously this doesn't answer all the questions about Church and State, but the principle is clear: it's right to show allegiance to the state, but it's also true that allegiance to God matters.

Jesus may be saying something else, too. Just as we owe the coin to Caesar because his image is on it, so we owe our *selves* to God because his image is on us (see Gen 1:27 and James 3:9b).

Here are religious leaders who have never given themselves to God. No wonder *they were amazed* (22).

2. Marriage at the resurrection (23-33)

Now it is the Sadducees who come with a trick question. It's about one of their favourite subjects: they don't believe there is life after death (see 23).

Their funny story is about a woman who marries seven brothers one after the other, according to the levirate law in the book of Deuteronomy (24-27, and see Deut 25:5-6).

So they ask Jesus *Whose wife will she be of the seven, since all of them were married to her?* (28)

The question earns them a strong rebuke: *You are in error because you do not know the Scriptures or the power of God* (29). Jesus is not pulling his punches: he is being as blunt with the Sadducees as he had been with the Pharisees and the Herodians.

Section Five: The Judge (Matthew 19:3 – 26:2)

Jesus goes on to say two things.

First, he explains that there will be no marriage in heaven (see 30). And, *second*, because the Sadducees only accept the authority of the five books of Moses, he proves the reality of life after death from the book of Exodus.

After quoting God's words to Moses from the burning bush (32a, see also Exod 3:6), Jesus concludes that God *is not the God of the dead but of the living* (32b).

To that the Sadducees have no answer.

3. – The greatest commandment (34-40)

An expert in the law (35) asks a question as spokesman for all the Pharisees: *Teacher, which is the greatest commandment in the Law?* (36)

Jesus replies by choosing two: *Love the Lord your God with all your heart and with all your soul and with all your mind* (37, quoting Deut 6:5) and *Love your neighbour as yourself* (39, quoting Lev 19:18).

All the Law and the Prophets, says Jesus, *hang on these two commandments* (40): the other commandments depend on these.

In replying to the third trick question Jesus has not gone on the attack.

But he does it now, *while the Pharisees were gathered together* (41). If the religious leaders call the Messiah *the Son of David*, why is it that in the Psalms David refers to the Messiah as his *Lord* (see 42-45, and also Ps 110:1)?

The answer, of course, is that the Messiah is, in one person, the human son of David and the divine Lord of David. But Matthew leaves us to work this out for ourselves.

At the end of the narrative part of Section Five Jesus is pointing unmistakeably to his own identity, and using unanswerable arguments to do it.

No wonder Matthew tells us that *no one dared to ask him any more questions* (46b). What we have been reading about Jesus may prompt us to worship him.

Teaching (23:1 – 26:2)

Jesus goes on to explain how he will come as Judge.

He will come to judge the religious leadership of Israel. And, one day, he will come again in glory as the Judge of all humankind.

A. Judgment on the scribes and the Pharisees (23:1-39)

1. – Warning about the scribes and the Pharisees (1-12)

Here Jesus is talking to *the crowds and to the disciples* (1); he mentions two signs that the leaders are on the wrong path.

First, *they do not practise what they preach* (3b). In principle it is fine to *do everything they tell you* (3a) because as the teachers of God's law they *sit in Moses' seat* (2).

But they themselves don't live according to this law. In telling others to obey it *they tie up heavy, cumbersome loads and put them on other people's shoulders* (4a), but they don't help or *lift a finger to move them* (4b).

And second, *everything they do is done for people to see* (5a, and see also chapter 6:1ff).

The scribes and the Pharisees are not looking for praise from God but from people: they dress to impress (see 5b), they want *the most important seats in the synagogues* (6b) and they want to be called *Rabbi* (7).

It's all for show.

But now Jesus is focusing on his disciples and warning them that they are not to adopt this status-seeking attitude: *But you are not to be called 'Rabbi', for you have one Teacher* (8). He makes the same point with the words *father* and *instructor* (see 9-10).

This jockeying for position is wrong because they are *all brothers* (8b) and because they have *one Instructor, the Messiah* (10b).

Anyone who doesn't recognise that, is not really a disciple of Jesus.

So the warning, both to the crowds and to the disciples, is blunt: the religious leaders are not an example to follow.

2. – Condemnation of the scribes and the Pharisees (13-36)

Now Jesus is no longer talking *about* the religious leaders: he is talking *to* them. And he is denouncing their attitudes and their behaviour.

Jesus does this in a series of accusations, each beginning *Woe to you…*

The background to this is in Old Testament prophecy. We have already seen that the parable of the tenants gets its vineyard picture for Israel from the book of Isaiah (see my comments on chapter 21:33; see also Isa 5:2,7).

But in that same chapter of Isaiah we read a series of six denunciations of the people of Israel, each beginning *Woe…* (see Isa 5:8,11,18,20,21,22).

Section Five: The Judge (Matthew 19:3 – 26:2)   133

So now here is Jesus condemning the religious leadership of Israel.

The first woe (13): You're preventing people from knowing God! The scribes and the Pharisees are *hypocrites* (13): they *shut the door of the kingdom of heaven in people's faces* (13).

And they don't even enter the kingdom themselves.

The second woe (15): You're wrong and you're converting people to your wrongness! These leaders put in so much effort *to win a single convert* (15), says Jesus.

But feel the force of what he says next: then *you make them twice as much a child of hell as you are* (15).

The third woe (16-22): Your clever discussions just show how blind you are! The religious leaders love talking about which oaths are binding and which aren't.

Here's one example: *If anyone swears by the temple, it means nothing; but anyone who swears by the gold of the temple is bound by that oath* (16). And Jesus gives another example too (see 18 and chapter 5:33-35).

But, says Jesus, every oath ultimately involves God: *Anyone who swears by the temple swears by it and by the one who dwells in it* (21, see also 22).

So these nit-picking discussions simply reveal what the scribes and the Pharisees are really like: they are *blind guides* (16), *blind fools* (17) and *blind men* (19).

The fourth woe (23-24): You're missing the main thing! These leaders pay a lot of attention to obeying the tithing laws: *you give a tenth of your spices – mint, dill and cumin* (23a).

Jesus is not knocking that. But, he says, *you have neglected the more important matters of the law – justice, mercy and faithfulness* (23b). They *should have practised the latter, without neglecting the former* (23b).

The main thing is the command to love God and our neighbour (see chapter 22:34-40 and 19:19). But the scribes and the Pharisees are missing this completely.

Jesus uses a funny picture to make a serious point: *You strain out a gnat but swallow a camel* (24). No wonder he calls them, once again, *blind guides* (24).

The fifth woe (25-26): You don't understand what righteousness is! The scribes and the Pharisees think being righteous is about *looking* good on the outside, and that the heart doesn't matter.

So they *clean the outside of the cup and dish, but inside they are full of greed and self-indulgence* (25b).

The leaders, says Jesus, are *blind* (26) and *hypocrites* (25). They fail to see that God is looking for a deeper righteousness (see chapter 5:20 and 15:11,18-20).

The sixth woe (27-28): You look righteous but you aren't! The scribes and the Pharisees look good, but that doesn't reflect the reality of the situation.

Jesus spells it out: *On the outside you appear to people as righteous but on the inside you are full of hypocrisy and wickedness* (28). They are like tombs with decaying bodies inside but which *look beautiful on the outside* (27).

The seventh woe (29-36): You say you're better than your ancestors, but you aren't! These leaders know that many of the Old Testament prophets were persecuted, but they maintain that they themselves are innocent.

Jesus knows what they're saying: *If we had lived in the days of our ancestors, we would not have taken part with them in shedding the blood of the prophets* (30).

But now he rounds on them and tells them to *Go ahead, then, and complete what your ancestors started!* (32)

This is strong stuff. But Jesus is not finished with them yet.

The scribes and the Pharisees are involved in the guilt of their forefathers (see 31) and they will continue their wickedness when he sends them more prophets and teachers: *Some of them you will kill and crucify; others you will flog in your synagogues and pursue from town to town* (34b).

So these leaders are doubly guilty, and so deserve to be condemned, says Jesus: *Upon you will come all the righteous blood that has been shed on earth* (35a).

When he adds *from the blood of righteous Abel to the blood of Zechariah son of Berekiah* (35b), Jesus is talking about the first and the last martyrs of the Old Testament (see Gen 4:10 and 2 Chr 24:20-22 [2 Chronicles was the last book of the Jewish Bible]).

It's worth noticing that during this final woe Jesus calls these leaders *snakes* and a *brood of vipers* (33a): John the Baptist used the same language about the Pharisees and the Sadducees back in Section One (see chapter 3:7).

We saw earlier that the background to Jesus' denunciation of Israel's leaders is Isaiah chapter 5 with its six woes. But now Jesus has pronounced *seven* woes over the scribes and the Pharisees.

Seven is the number of completeness, so the message is clear.

Jesus' condemnation here means that God's judgment can no longer be delayed: *Truly I tell you, all this will come upon this generation* (36).

We can only imagine how the scribes and the Pharisees feel when Jesus asks them this question: *How will you escape being condemned to hell?* (33)

3. – Bad news for the scribes and the Pharisees (37-39)

When Jesus calls out *Jerusalem, Jerusalem, you who kill the prophets and stone those sent to you* (37a), he is using the capital city as a symbol for the whole nation.

A tender image expresses his desire to bring Israel to repentance: *How often have I longed to gather your children together, as a hen gathers her chicks under her wings* (37b). That's the story of Jesus' preaching and miracles.

But the tragedy is that *you were not willing* (37b).

And now Jesus, who came preaching the good news of the kingdom of God, announces bad news: *Look, your house is left to you desolate* (38).

Jesus is talking about what will happen to the temple in Jerusalem, as chapter 24 will make clear. The temple is the symbol of God's relationship with his people: when the people don't want the relationship, the temple is abandoned.

In order to repent, Israel would need to say, as a nation, what the crowds shouted when Jesus entered the city on a donkey: *Blessed is he who comes in the name of the Lord* (39; see also chapter 21:9 and Ps 118:26).

But this is not a promise that they will.

The message of judgment on Israel in this Gospel has sounded loud and clear (see chapter 8:11-12; 12:38-45; 21:40-43; 22:7; 23:32-36).

This is bad news for the scribes and the Pharisees: God's judgment is coming.

Now Jesus goes on to explain what that will look like.

Introduction to chapters 24 and 25

After Jesus tells them that the temple will be destroyed (see chapter 24:2), the disciples have one question for him: *When will this happen, and what will be the sign of your coming and of the end of the age?* (chapter 24:3b)

They *think* it's one question, but actually it's *two*.

The disciples think it's one question because it seems obvious to them that the destruction of the temple and the end of the age are the same event: how could the world possibly continue if the temple were no longer standing?

The first question is *When will this happen?* and relates to the destruction of the temple which Jesus has just mentioned (see 2).

The second question is *What will be the sign of your coming and of the end of the age?* and relates to Jesus' return in glory at the end of human history.

Jesus' reply teaches the disciples that they have asked two questions and that these apply to two separate events.

Both of which demonstrate that God's judgment is at work.

(For other approaches to the interpretation of these chapters, see the longer commentaries; and see also Appendix 1, Question 5.)

B. Judgment in the fall of Jerusalem (24:1-35)

Jesus points to the temple and tells the disciples that *not one stone here will be left on another; every one will be thrown down* (2).

So, as we have already seen, the disciples ask Jesus *When will this happen, and what will be the sign of your coming and of the end of the age?* (3b)

Jesus is going to answer their first question, which is *When will this happen?* This is about the destruction of the temple.

1. – The end is not yet (4-8)

Jesus tells the disciples to *watch out that no one deceives you* (4). There will be false messiahs (see 5) and *wars and rumours of wars* (6a).

But they are not to jump to conclusions: *Such things must happen, but the end is still to come* (6b).

And Jesus says it again: *All these are the beginning of birth-pains* (8).

When a woman goes into labour, the birth of her baby is still in the future. In other words: the end is not yet.

2. – How to live in the meantime (9-14)

This time, says Jesus, will be characterised by persecution, hatred, betrayal and deception (see 9-11, and compare chapter 10:17-22).

And he adds that *because of the increase of wickedness, the love of most will grow cold* (12).

But Jesus' disciples are to be different because they know that *the one who stands firm to the end will be saved* (13): they won't give up and will experience God's blessing.

And now Jesus makes clear that his prohibition of telling Gentiles the good news (see chapter 10:5-6 and 15:24) was only temporary: *This gospel of the kingdom will be preached in the whole world as a testimony to all nations* (14).

This is how his disciples are to live: standing firm and strong in love.

Then, says Jesus, talking about the destruction of the temple, *the end will come* (14b).

3. – How to recognise the Judean crisis (15-28)

Jesus explains that a repeat of *the abomination that causes desolation* mentioned in the prophecy of Daniel (see Dan 9:27; 11:31; 12:11), which will happen *in the holy place* (15), will signal that the crisis in Judea has kicked off.

This is referring to the Jewish War of AD 66-70, when the Romans would come to ravage the farmlands and villages of Judea.

So people are to run for their lives (see 16), with no time to collect valuables (see 17-18). *How dreadful it will be in those days,* says Jesus, *for pregnant women and nursing mothers!* (19)

The whole period will be one of *great distress* (21), so great that *for the sake of the elect those days will be shortened* (22).

And Jesus repeats his warning about *false messiahs and false prophets* (24): twice he says *Do not believe it* (23b, 26b).

The reason is simple. When the Son of Man finally intervenes, it will be unmistakeable: *For as lightning that comes from the east is visible even in the west, so will be the coming of the Son of Man* (27).

Just as the presence of vultures points to the fact that there's a corpse (see 28), so the intervention of the Son of Man will be obvious to those with eyes to see.

4. – The temple's destruction and the Son's triumph (29-31)

When we hear Jesus talking about his *coming* (27b), our thoughts naturally turn to his Second Coming in glory at the end of human history.

But that cannot be what is in view here: Jesus will soon say that *this generation will not pass away until all these things have happened* (34).

So the coming Jesus is talking about here is a coming in judgment within the lifetime of many of his listeners: he is answering the first of the disciples' two questions, which is about the destruction of the temple (see 2-3).

To communicate the enormity of this, Jesus doesn't mention the temple by name but uses the symbolic language of apocalyptic: *The sun will be darkened, and the moon will not give its light; the stars will fall from the sky, and the heavenly bodies will be shaken* (29, and see Isa 13:10).

Now Jesus talks about *the Son of Man coming on the clouds of heaven, with power and great glory* (30b): as we have already seen, this refers to Daniel's prophecy (see Dan 7:13-14), which is about the Son of Man coming *to* God and not *from* God.

In other words, this coming is about the exaltation of Jesus in his ascension back into his Father's presence.

So the apocalyptic language makes two things clear: the temple is destroyed as an act of divine judgment, and Jesus the Son is vindicated over the Jewish leadership which has rejected him.

And the Son, says Jesus, will bring his people home. This will happen as the good news of the kingdom of God is preached around the world (see 31).

5. – Jesus' answer to the disciples' first question (32-35)

Just as the disciples know that summer is near when they see figs on the fig-tree (see 32), *even so, when you see all **these things**, you know that it is near* (33): Jesus is referring to the destruction of the temple.

And this is going to happen within the lifetime of many of his listeners: *Truly I tell you, this generation will certainly not pass away until all **these things** have happened* (34).

It is worth noticing that Jesus uses the expression **these things** in verse 33 and in verse 34. This links back directly to the disciples' first question

Section Five: The Judge (Matthew 19:3 – 26:2)

about when the temple will be destroyed: *When will **these things** happen?* (3, literal translation).

We can look back to the destruction of the Jerusalem temple in AD 70, when Jesus came in judgment to demonstrate his victory.

But there is another, final, coming of Jesus to which we still look forward.

And he wants his disciples then, and us now, to know that what he is teaching is true: *Heaven and earth will pass away,* says Jesus, *but my words will never pass away* (35).

C. Judgment at the return of Jesus (24:36 – 25:46)

Now the focus changes, from the destruction of the temple to Jesus' return in glory. The contrast between verse 34 and verse 36 makes this clear.

So now Jesus is answering the second of the disciples' two questions (see 3b).

1. – His coming: unpredictable and inescapable (24:36-41)

Jesus doesn't know when his return in glory is going to be: *But about that day or hour no one knows, not even the angels in heaven, nor the Son, but only the Father* (36).

He explains what it will be like *at the coming of the Son of Man* (37) by comparing it with the experience of the contemporaries of Noah, who *knew nothing about what would happen until the flood came and took them all away* (39).

That, says Jesus, *is how it will be at the coming of the Son of Man* (39b).

This unpreparedness will result in disaster: *Two women will be grinding with a hand mill; one will be taken and the other left* (41, see also 40).

So it is clear what topic Jesus will turn to now.

2. – Our readiness (24:42 – 25:30)

Jesus is going to underline the importance of our being ready for his return by telling three parables.

But first he stresses the principle: *Therefore keep watch, because you do not know on what day your Lord will come* (42).

A thief doesn't advertise the time of his arrival (see 43); in the same way *you also must be ready, because the Son of Man will come at an hour when you do not expect him* (44).

So all three parables are about being ready for the day Jesus comes back in glory.

a. the parable of the servant put in charge (24:45-51). A rich man is going away, so gives one of his servants the responsibility to look after the household in his absence.

But then one day he comes home.

If the master discovers that the servant has taken his responsibility seriously, there will be a reward: *he will put him in charge of all his possessions* (47).

But if the servant has taken the opportunity *to beat his fellow servants and to eat and drink with drunkards* (49), punishment awaits him (see 51).

Here's the principle again: the master will *come on a day when he does not expect him and at an hour he is not aware of* (50).

Being ready for Jesus' return means living in obedience to him by serving others, like *the faithful and wise servant* in the parable (45).

Jesus is asking us the question: *Are you ready?*

b. the parable of the girls waiting for the bridegroom (25:1-13). Just as the master in the first parable represented Jesus, so the bridegroom here represents him too.

This is a bold move on Jesus' part: the Old Testament often describes *God* as the bridegroom, but never *the Messiah*. But now, once again (see my comments on chapter 9:15), he is using the word to describe himself.

The ten girls have the task of taking their lamps with them to welcome the bridegroom (see 1).

Five of them are foolish because they *did not take any oil with them* (3), while the five wise girls *took oil in jars along with their lamps* (4).

Now Jesus tells us that *the bridegroom was a long time in coming* (5a). The interesting thing is that the girls *all became drowsy and fell asleep* (5b): in other words, *none of them* knows the time of the bridegroom's arrival (and see chapter 24:36).

When the bridegroom arrives the foolish girls ask the others for some of their oil (see 6-8), but the answer is No: *There may not be enough for both us and you* (9).

The message is clear: no one can rely on someone else's preparedness. We need to be ready *ourselves*.

What makes this all the more important is the fact that that there is such a thing as being too late: when the foolish girls finally turn up, having gone to buy some oil, *the door was shut* (10b).

And the bridegroom tells them *I don't know you* (12).

This detail doesn't really fit the story: instead, the parable's meaning is creeping into the parable itself. If we are not ready for the return of Jesus we show that we have never really been in relationship with him at all (see also chapter 7:23).

Jesus is asking us the question again: *Are you ready?*

What being ready involves will become clearer when we read the third parable. But Jesus sums up his message: *Therefore keep watch, because you do not know the day or the hour* (13, see also chapter 24:42).

c. the parable of the servants given lots of money (25:14-30). Once again, a master is going away, so *he called his servants and entrusted his wealth to them* (14).

NIV2011 doesn't use the word *talents* for this money, but *bags of gold* (15), presumably to avoid the confusion with our word for an aptitude or ability. The important thing is that the sums involved are huge: a talent was worth 20 years' wages.

The master gives each servant money *according to his ability* (15b).

The servant given five bags *gained five bags more* (16) and the one with two bags *gained two more* (17). They have put their master's money to work.

But the servant given one bag *went off, dug a hole in the ground and hid his master's money* (18).

The master comes home *after a long time* (19).

The servant who now has ten bags of gold instead of his original five is congratulated by his master: *Well done, good and faithful servant!* (21a)

He is rewarded, too: *You have been faithful with a few things; I will put you in charge of many things* (21).

And the same thing happens to the servant originally given two bags of gold (see 22-23).

Now the servant with one bag of gold steps forward. He tells his master *I was afraid and went out and hid your gold in the ground* (25). The reason he gives is that *I knew that you are a hard man, harvesting where you have not sown and gathering where you have not scattered seed* (24).

Jesus doesn't mean this as a description of himself: it's simply a detail in the story.

The master seems happy to accept the servant's description of him (see 26), but adds that *you should have put my money on deposit with the bankers* (27).

And now the meaning of the parable once again invades the story: the master gives orders to *throw that worthless servant outside, into the darkness, where there will be weeping and gnashing of teeth* (30).

Being ready for Jesus doesn't mean doing the minimum; it means living a life of active, faithful service.

So the question comes again: *Are you ready?*

3. – His judgment: final and authoritative (25:31-46)

We have seen that the theme of judgment has been there throughout Section Five, but especially in its teaching part.

Now, as we come to Judgment Day, we reach the climax.

This is not a parable, but a description of the final judgment and the basis for it. What is immediately striking is that the judge is Jesus himself.

There will be a day *when the Son of Man comes in his glory, and all the angels with him* (31); *he will sit on his glorious throne* (31b, see also chapter 19:28 and John 5:19-29).

Gathered before him will be *all the nations* (32a), in other words the Gentile nations and Israel too.

And Jesus makes clear that he is going *to separate the people one from another* (32) by reminding his listeners of a shepherd separating sheep and goats: those who are sheep he will put on his right, and those who are goats he will put on his left (see 32b-33).

Jesus, who is the Son of Man, the King (see 34, 40) and the Judge, will deal with both groups as he delivers his final and authoritative judgment.

First, the King speaks to those on his right (34-40). He begins with the words *Come, you who are blessed by my Father* (34). He tells them to *take your inheritance* (34).

Section Five: The Judge (Matthew 19:3 – 26:2) 143

Jesus tells them that the reason is that *I was hungry and you gave me something to eat, I was thirsty and you gave me something to drink, I was a stranger and you invited me in* (35).

But there is more: *I needed clothes and you clothed me, I was ill and you looked after me, I was in prison and you came to visit me* (36).

The people the King is talking to are puzzled: they don't remember helping him when he was hungry, thirsty, lonely, poor, sick or in prison (see 37-39).

Now Jesus explains what he means: *Whatever you did for one of the least of these brothers and sisters of mine, you did for me* (40).

Jesus is *not* saying that being kind gets us into heaven. And he has already made clear that the inheritance awaiting these people on his right was *prepared for you since the creation of the world* (34b).

What Jesus *is* saying is that our behaviour to his followers (*these brothers and sisters of mine*, 40) reveals our attitude to Jesus himself. This is a principle we have already met in this Gospel (see chapter 10:40,42).

Second, the King speaks to those on his left (41-46). He begins with condemnation: *Depart from me, you who are cursed, into the eternal fire* (41a).

It is interesting that the fires of hell were not originally intended for human beings: this fire was *prepared for the devil and his angels* (41b).

The reason for this condemnation is these people's refusal to help him when he was hungry, thirsty, lonely, poor, sick or in prison (see 42-43).

Here, too, there is puzzlement: *When did we see you hungry or thirsty or a stranger or needing clothes or ill or in prison, and did not help you?* (44)

The King's answer, says Jesus, will be as follows: *Whatever you did not do for one of the least of these, you did not do for me* (45).

Jesus is still talking about what people have done, or not done, for *these brothers and sisters of mine* (40). The principle is clear: our behaviour to the followers of Jesus reveals our attitude to Jesus himself.

No one gets to heaven by being kind, but by being in relationship with Jesus. But if I am not kind to Jesus-followers, I am showing that I do not know him.

The climax of Section Five's teaching part is very solemn. There is going to be a Judgment Day, where Jesus the Judge will make a separation. Some will go to heaven, while others will go to hell (see 46).

And the basis on which Jesus will make that decision is our behaviour towards those who follow him. If we know him ourselves, we will be kind to his followers; if we don't, we won't.

So closely does Jesus identify himself with those who follow him, that he can say to people that *whatever you did for one of the least of these brothers and sisters of mine, you did for me* (40).

Now Matthew signals that the end of Section Five is upon us, by using a phrase we have become used to: *When Jesus had finished saying all these things...* (chapter 26:1a, see also chapter 7:28; 11:1; 13:53; 19:1).

We have witnessed Jesus the Judge arriving in Jerusalem.

Now, says Matthew, *he said to his disciples, 'As you know, the Passover is two days away – and the Son of Man will be handed over to be crucified'* (chapter 26:1b-2).

So Section Five ends with Jesus predicting his suffering, death and resurrection for a fourth time (see also chapter 16:21; 17:22-23; 20:17-19). And *now* he links it with the Jewish Passover Feast.

The stage is set for the dramatic events of Section Six.

Learning the Gospel

Section Five covers seven chapters of Matthew's Gospel, so learning the order of the events may seem like a tall order.

But in fact Section Five is one of the easiest to learn.

Start with the narrative part, learning just the main headings in bold. A, B, C, E, F and G are all in groups of three; only D is a single event (*Jesus enters Jerusalem*).

When you can say those seven headings easily from memory, start to learn the sub-headings: if you do it aloud you will find this much easier than you expect.

Now turn to the teaching part of the section. Learn the three main headings (in bold) first: this will be no problem. Then go back and learn the sub-headings.

As you commit Section Five to memory, you will find yourself remembering all sorts of details.

Section Five: The Judge
Narrative

A. Three issues Jesus addresses
   1. Marriage
   2. Children
   3. Possessions

B. Three rewards Jesus promises
   1. Disciples will share his victory
   2. Disciples will gain more than they give up
   3. Disciples will experience the surprises of the new age

C. Three things Jesus does *before* entering Jerusalem
   1. Jesus' third prediction
   2. The Zebedee family request
   3. The healing of two blind men

D. Jesus enters Jerusalem
   1. What Jesus does
   2. What the crowd shouts
   3. What everyone asks

E. Three things Jesus does *after* entering Jerusalem
   1. He clears the temple
   2. He curses the fig-tree
   3. He confuses the religious leaders

F. Three parables Jesus tells
   1. The two sons
   2. The tenants
   3. The wedding banquet

G. Three traps Jesus avoids
   1. Paying taxes to Caesar
   2. Marriage at the resurrection
   3. The greatest commandment

Teaching

A. Judgment on the scribes and the Pharisees
   1. Warning about the scribes and the Pharisees

2. Condemnation of the scribes and the Pharisees
   3. Bad news for the scribes and the Pharisees
B. Judgment in the fall of Jerusalem
   1. The end is not yet
   2. How to live in the meantime
   3. How to recognise the Judean crisis
   4. The temple's destruction and the Son's triumph
   5. Jesus' answer to the disciples' first question
C. Judgment at the return of Jesus
   1. His coming: unpredictable and inescapable
   2. Our readiness
      a. the parable of the servant put in charge
      b. the parable of the girls waiting for the bridegroom
      c. the parable of the servants given lots of money
   3. His judgment: final and authoritative

'When Jesus had finished...'

Meeting the Lord

As you tell yourself the incidents in the narrative part of Section Five, or meet up with a friend to do this together, fill in as many details as you can call to mind.

And talk to the Lord about what you are remembering. Tell him your reaction to what he says about marriage, children and possessions; then thank him for the rewards he promises to disciples.

And so on through the whole narrative part.

Now do the same thing with the teaching part of the section. You won't get all the details, but you will find yourself thanking Jesus for the certainty of his return in glory one day.

And asking him to help you to be ready to welcome him.

This is so worth it: as you do this, you will be meeting the Lord. Enjoy!

Section Six: The Lover
Matthew 26:3 – 28:20

The whole Gospel has been leading up to this section: now we are arriving at the climax of the story Matthew has to tell. In Section Six we will meet betrayal, anguish, confusion, fear and despair, but most of all we will see love. We will see the depth of Jesus' love at the cross and its triumph at the empty tomb. This is holy ground.

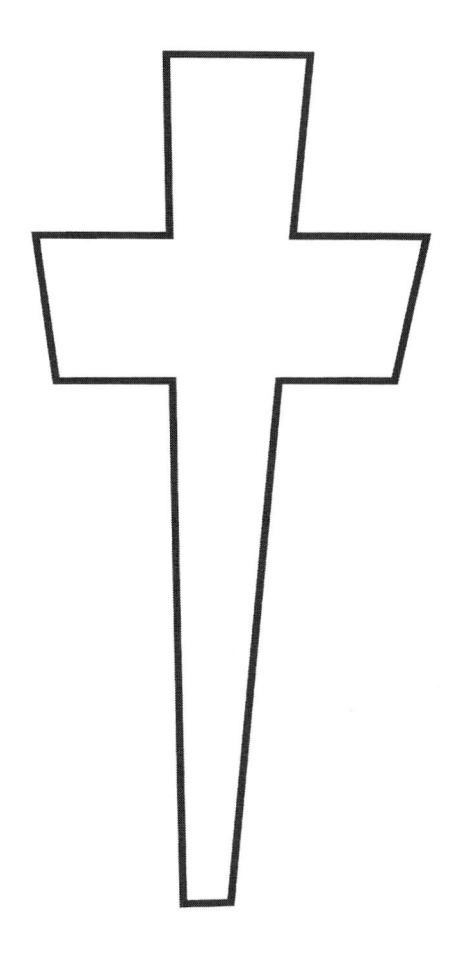

Then they led him away to crucify him.

Matthew 27:31b

Enjoying the View

Narrative (26:3 – 28:20)

Block A (26:3-16)

a. Plans against Jesus (3-5)
b. The anointing at Bethany (6-13)
c'. Plans against Jesus (14-16)

Block B (26:17 – 27:56)

a. The last supper (26:17-30)
b. Jesus predicts Peter's denial (26:31-35)
c. Gethsemane (26:36-46)
d. Jesus arrested (26:47-56)
d'. Before the Jewish Council (26:57-68)
c'. Peter denies Jesus (26:69-75)
b'. Jesus before Pilate (and Judas hangs himself) (27:1-26)
a'. The crucifixion (27:27-56)

Block C (27:57 – 28:20)

a. Jesus: dead and buried (27:57-61)
b. The guards at the tomb (27:62-66)
c. The empty tomb and the risen Jesus (28:1-10)
b'. The guards' report (28:11-15)
a'. Jesus: sovereign and sending (28:16-20)

All three incident blocks in Section Six have mirror links. This means that a and a' have something in common and b and b' have something in common, and so on.

In Block A, the anointing at Bethany is sandwiched between the plans of Jesus' enemies to do away with him, so there is a powerful pattern of hate-love-hate.

And in Block C the message of the resurrection is at the centre of everything (incident c), and the transformation of Jesus from a dead body (incident a) to the sending king (incident a') shows his victory, despite the strategies of his opponents (b and b').

As well as having mirror links, Block B's incidents are grouped in pairs. After the last supper Jesus predicts that Peter will deny him (incidents a and b); Jesus prays in Gethsemane and is then arrested there (incidents c

Section Six: The Lover (Matthew 26:3 – 28:20)   149

and d); while Jesus is being cross-examined by the high priest, Peter is denying his master in the courtyard outside (incidents d' and c'); and Jesus' trial before the Roman governor leads to his crucifixion by Roman soldiers (incidents b' and a').

(For a brief summary of all the mirror links in Section Six, see Appendix 2.)

Please take time to read through Section Six at one sitting: you may even like to read it aloud. Much of it will be familiar. But try to imagine the scene and the emotions of all those who have anything to do with Jesus.

As you read, you may find yourself stopping to worship.

Unpacking the Content

Narrative (26:3 – 28:20)
Block A (26:3-16)

a. – Plans against Jesus (3-5)

This is the beginning of the sandwich which contrasts the hatred of the Jewish leaders, and then of Judas (see 3-5, 14-16), with the love of one woman (see 6-13).

Most people are in Jerusalem to celebrate Passover to thank God for rescuing Israel from slavery in Egypt, but the leaders have something else on their minds: *they schemed to arrest Jesus secretly and kill him* (4).

But they are careful. They don't want to do it during Passover, *or there may be a riot among the people* (5).

b. – The anointing at Bethany (6-13)

The woman here is Mary, the sister of Lazarus (see John 12:1-11), but Matthew doesn't tell us her name: he wants us to focus not on her identity but on her love.

The perfume she pours over Jesus is *very expensive* (7): when the disciples see what she is doing *they were indignant* (8).

But Jesus springs to her defence and describes her action in four ways.

First, it is *beautiful* (10). Second, it is right: *the poor you will always have with you, but you will not always have me* (11).

Third, it is prophetic: in pouring out her perfume, *she did it to prepare me for burial* (12). Usually you anoint a body after its owner has died, but somehow this woman senses that Jesus is soon to go to his death: this moves her to this prophetic act of love.

And, fourth, it is unforgettable: Jesus adds that *wherever this gospel is preached throughout the world, what she has done will also be told, in memory of her* (13).

It's like Jesus is guaranteeing that this incident will be part of the New Testament.

It's not hard to see why this woman's extravagant act of love is so important to Jesus. He has come to Jerusalem as the heavenly Lover to perform the most extravagant act of love the world will ever see.

He will die on the cross for our sins.

a'. – Plans against Jesus (14-16)

Jesus' defence of the woman seems to have been the last straw for Judas, who goes *to the chief priests* with an offer they can't refuse (14). He wants to know what they will give him *if I deliver him over to you* (15).

With his offer he earns himself *thirty pieces of silver* (15b, and see Zech 11:12).

Matthew has gone to the trouble to tell us that Judas is *one of the Twelve* (14), which highlights the enormity of the betrayal. So one of Jesus' close team *watched for an opportunity to hand him over* (16).

Block B (26:17 – 27:56)

a. – The last supper (26:17-30)

The mirror structure in Block B links this incident with the crucifixion, and the connection is not hard to find: incident a explains incident a'. The events of the last supper explain the meaning of Jesus' death.

Matthew reminds us that this is going to be a Passover meal, and shows us that Jesus has gone to great lengths to make the practical arrangements (see 17-19).

At the meal Jesus explains to the disciples that *one of you will betray me* (21); for this man *it would be better for him if he had not been born* (24b).

Jesus makes clear, too, that *the Son of Man will go just as it is written about him* (24a): this betrayal, and the death it will lead to, are part of Old Testament prophecy (see, for example, Ps 41:9; Isa 52:13 – 53:12).

Section Six: The Lover (Matthew 26:3 – 28:20)

Judas, along with the other disciples, asks Jesus if *he* is the betrayer, to which Jesus replies *You have said so* (25): presumably the others don't hear this exchange as they are talking to one another at the time.

Now Jesus gives the disciples the bread and the wine which were part of every Passover celebration.

After first giving them the bread (*Take and eat; this is my body*, 26), Jesus gives them the cup. His words are significant: *This is my blood of the covenant* (28a).

There were Old Testament promises that God would one day establish a new covenant in which men and women would find forgiveness in a relationship with God (see Jer 31:31-34) and experience the presence of the Holy Spirit (see Ezek 36:26-27).

Now Jesus is saying that his death will make that covenant possible.

And he spells it out: his blood *is poured out for many for the forgiveness of sins* (28). He will die so that others can come into relationship with God.

In verse 29 Jesus looks beyond his death by referring to the messianic banquet in heaven one day (see my comments on chapter 14:15-21).

b. – Jesus predicts Peter's denial (26:31-35)

First, Jesus predicts that all the disciples will desert him, and he quotes from the Old Testament to prove it: through the prophet Zechariah God says *I will strike the shepherd, and the sheep of the flock will be scattered* (31b, and see Zech 13:7).

This should stop us in our tracks. The death of Jesus will not only be the result of the actions of the Jews and the Romans, but of God himself.

This desertion will not be forever, says Jesus: *After I have risen, I will go ahead of you into Galilee* (32).

Peter is sure that he will never let Jesus down (see 33). But Jesus warns him: *This very night, before the cock crows, you will disown me three times* (34).

What Peter says now is stupid, but understandable because he loves Jesus: *Even if I have to die with you, I will never disown you* (35).

c. – Gethsemane (26:36-46)

Jesus takes Peter, James and John with him to a garden called Gethsemane: he tells them *My soul is overwhelmed with sorrow to the point of death* (38).

Telling them to keep watch Jesus goes further into the garden and *fell with his face to the ground* (39a): his body language speaks volumes. He prays *My Father, if it is possible, may this cup be taken from me* (39).

The cup is a picture for suffering God's punishment for sin (see, for example, Isa 51:17). Jesus is shrinking from what is in front of him, not simply from the physical pain but also from the spiritual cost: he will take the divine judgment onto himself which others deserve.

But through it all Jesus remains in submission to his Father: *Yet not as I will, but as you will* (39b).

Returning to the three disciples Jesus wakes them and warns them to *watch and pray so that you will not fall into temptation* (41). And he tells them *why* this is so important: *the spirit is willing, but the flesh is weak* (41b).

None of them is going to heed his warning.

Jesus prays his prayer twice more, but each time the disciples fail to keep awake. And three times the answer is No: there is no other way for sinners to be saved.

And so, at the end of the paragraph Jesus goes to meet his betrayer (see 46). He has made his decision.

d. – Jesus arrested (26:47-56)

Matthew wants to emphasize Jesus' loneliness: Judas is *one of the Twelve* (47). He arrives in Gethsemane with a crowd of armed men and a kiss of betrayal (see 48-49).

In response to Jesus' arrest, one of the disciples resorts to violence in order to engineer an escape (51, and see John 18:10).

Jesus tells him to stop, because he could escape at any time: *Do you think I cannot call on my Father, and he will at once put at my disposal more than twelve legions of angels?* (53)

But Jesus makes clear that he is committed to obeying his Father: if he escaped, *how then would the Scriptures be fulfilled that say it must happen in this way?* (54)

And now he says the same to the crowd who have arrested him: *This has all taken place that the writings of the prophets might be fulfilled* (56).

This is the moment when Jesus' loneliness becomes even more intense. Matthew tells us that *all the disciples deserted him and fled* (56b). And these are not his enemies: they are his best friends.

Section Six: The Lover (Matthew 26:3 – 28:20)   153

d'. – Before the Jewish Council (26:57-68)

There is an extra sandwich which starts here in verse 58 and ends in verse 75. By mentioning Peter before we hear Jesus' cross-examination before the Council, Matthew makes clear that incidents d' and c' are happening at the same time: while Jesus is being interrogated by the high priest, his friend is denying all knowledge of him.

With his mirror structure Matthew draws our attention to the contrast between Jesus' courage here in incident d' and the disciples' cowardice in running away at his arrest (incident d).

We are left in no doubt that Jesus is innocent, because those who bring so-called evidence against Jesus are *false witnesses* (60).

When the high priest begins his interrogation, Jesus doesn't defend himself but *remained silent* (63a). But then it comes to a direct question about his identity.

Putting him under oath, the high priest commands Jesus to *tell us if you are the Messiah, the Son of God* (63).

The reply *You have said so* (64a) means *You are right*, but Jesus goes on to make clear that he is not a political king but *the Son of Man sitting at the right hand of the Mighty One and coming on the clouds of heaven* (64).

The phrase *sitting at the right hand of the Mighty One* is an echo of Psalm 110:1 (and see chapter 22:33-34), while *coming on the clouds of heaven* has its background, as we have already seen, in Daniel 7:13-14.

Jesus' courage is astonishing: he must know that his claim to be the glorious *Son of Man* can only lead to his condemnation. His love for his Father and his love for sinners mean that he is determined to go to the cross.

And the high priest draws the obvious conclusion: *He has spoken blasphemy!* (65)

c'. – Peter denies Jesus (26:69-75)

By means of the mirror linking, Matthew makes a connection between this incident and the events in Gethsemane in incident c. There, Jesus had prayed three times; here, Peter denies him three times.

But there is another link too.

In Gethsemane Jesus had given the disciples a warning: *Watch and pray so that you will not fall into temptation* (41).

Now we see that Peter has not taken this warning to heart. While Jesus has been standing alone before the Jewish Council, he has been sitting in the courtyard outside (see 58 and 69). But three times he claims to have no connection with Jesus (see 70, 72, 74).

Matthew tells us that at the last denial Peter *began to call down curses* (74). Does this mean that he is cursing Jesus? Or it could be that he is saying something like *God curse me if I'm lying!*

Immediately Peter hears the cock crowing and remembers Jesus warning that he would deny him three times.

Then, says Matthew, *he went outside and wept bitterly* (75).

b'. – Jesus before Pilate (and Judas hangs himself) (27:1-26)

There is another sandwich here. Matthew begins his account of Jesus appearing before Pilate (1-2), but then breaks off to tell us about the fate of Judas (see 3-10).

So the mirror link between incidents b and b' is twofold.

First, there is a contrast between Peter and Judas, who are both unfaithful disciples. Peter promises Jesus that he is ready to die *with* him (see chapter 26:35), while Judas dies *without* him (see chapter 27:5).

And second, there is a contrast between the disloyalty of Peter (incident b) and the steadfastness of Jesus (incident b').

Judas, Matthew tells us, is *seized with remorse* (3): he gives back *the thirty pieces of silver to the chief priests and the elders* (3b) and tells them *I have sinned* (4a).

Judas seems to be very aware of his guilt: he knows that *I have betrayed innocent blood* (4a). But at the same time he has no hope. Matthew writes that *Judas threw the money into the temple and left. Then he went away and hanged himself* (5).

The chief priests use the money *to buy the potter's field as a burial place for foreigners* (7): Matthew sees these events as another fulfilment of Old Testament prophecy (see Zech 11:12-13; Jer 32:6-9).

Now we return to Jesus as he stands accused before Pilate (see 1-2 and 11).

Once again he refuses to defend himself (see 12-14), but once again he is open as to his identity (see 11b).

Pilate knows that *it was out of self-interest that they had handed Jesus over to him* (18), so he offers to release one prisoner *chosen by the crowd* (15).

Section Six: The Lover (Matthew 26:3 – 28:20)

But while he is making this offer he receives a message from his wife, who has had a disturbing dream in which Jesus has featured: she tells Pilate to not have *anything to do with that innocent man* (19).

We don't know what effect the message has on Pilate: perhaps he is hoping that the crowd will choose to have Jesus released rather than Barabbas.

But by now the crowd, encouraged by *the chief priests and the elders* (20) are shouting for Barabbas to be set free and for Jesus to be crucified (see 22).

Pilate asks *What crime has he committed?* (23) But *they shouted all the louder 'Crucify him!'* (23)

Pilate realises that he has lost the battle: he washes his hands and says to the crowd *I am innocent of this man's blood* (24b, and see the contrast with verse 4). And yet of course he is still responsible for his actions.

However, Pilate is telling the crowd that Jesus' death is their responsibility and not his (see 24b). Matthew writes: *All the people answered, 'His blood is on us and on our children!'* (25)

They are not calling down a curse on themselves, but acknowledging their responsibility for what is happening to Jesus. God would still love Israel, but the nation – as we have seen – is losing its privileged status (see my comments on chapter 21:43).

So Pilate does what the crowd have demanded from him: he has Jesus flogged, and *handed him over to be crucified* (26).

a'. – The crucifixion (27:27-56)

This final part of Block B is the climax to which Matthew has been bringing us. Jesus has predicted his own death (see chapter 16:21; 17:22-23; 20:17-19) and given brief insights into its meaning (see chapter 20:28; 26:1-2).

But we have had to wait until Section Six's account of the last supper for the fullest explanation (see chapter 26:26-30). The mirror structure linking incidents a and a' teaches us the meaning of the cross.

One way of looking at this passage is to examine the crucifixion itself, as well as what happens *before* it and *after* it.

First, before the crucifixion: mockery (see 27-31). Jesus is mocked by *the whole company of soldiers* (27).

The *scarlet robe* (28), the *crown of thorns* and the *staff in his right hand* (29) are a parody of the emperor's majesty: they kneel and call out *Hail, king of the Jews!* (29b)

Then the soldiers *put his own clothes on him* (31), before they *led him away to crucify him* (31b).

Second, the crucifixion itself (see 32-50). The *wine to drink, mixed with gall* (34) is probably an anaesthetic designed to reduce the pain of crucifixion.

But Jesus *refused to drink it* (34b): perhaps he is determined to be fully conscious as he suffers for our sins. And the charge above his head reads *This is Jesus, the king of the Jews* (37).

Matthew tells us that *two rebels were crucified with him* (38): these are political activists who had been committed to undermining the Romans.

But the mockery from the passers-by and from *the chief priests, the teachers of the law and the elders* (41) is aimed not at the three suffering men, but at Jesus specifically (see 39, 42-43).

The religious leaders remember that, although Jesus saved others, *he can't save himself!* (42a) The truth, of course, is somewhat different: it is *in order* to save others that he is not saving himself.

The mockery continues. If he is the Son of God and Israel's king, Jesus should *come down from the cross* (40, 42): *let God rescue him now if he wants him* (43).

And the rebels either side of Jesus *also heaped insults on him* (44).

Now Matthew tells us about three hours of darkness (see 45): is he wanting us to remember that darkness was the last plague in Egypt before the final event of the Passover (see Exod 10:21-23)?

After the three hours of darkness are over, Jesus cries out to God in Aramaic. So important is this that Matthew translates it for us: *My God, my God, why have you forsaken me?* (46)

There is only one thing in the universe which can separate a man or a woman from God, and that is human sin. But Jesus, as we have already seen, is entirely innocent.

This can only mean one thing: the sin separating Jesus from his Father is not *his*, but *ours*. An innocent man is dying in the place of guilty sinners.

Third, after the crucifixion: victory (see 51-56). As soon as Jesus dies (see 50), *the curtain of the temple was torn in two, from top to bottom* (51a).

The curtain before the Holy of Holies kept temple worshippers out of the presence of God: their sin made access to his holiness impossible.

Section Six: The Lover (Matthew 26:3 – 28:20)   157

But now the curtain has gone, because Jesus has died. The tearing of the curtain proclaims the victory of Jesus' death: it's like God is saying to anyone who will listen *You can come in now!*

This victory is confirmed by an earthquake (see 51b). Matthew tells us about tombs breaking open: *The bodies of many holy people who had died were raised to life* (52). But he adds that this happened *after Jesus' resurrection* (53).

Could this last detail be a clue that Matthew sees this historical event as happening in the future, as yet another confirmation of Jesus' victory on the cross?

The women who have followed Jesus are still there, *watching from a distance* (55).

But the reaction of *the centurion and those with him who were guarding Jesus* (54a) should stop us in our tracks again. They exclaim, says Matthew, *Surely he was the Son of God!* (54b)

We don't know how much they understood or what they meant by these words. But these are hardened soldiers, used to crucifixion. And they are *Gentiles*.

And Matthew surely wants us to recognise that the man on the cross is not just a tragic figure suffering an unjust death; he is the eternal Son of God, dying for the sins of the world.

Block C (27:57 – 28:20)

a. – Jesus: dead and buried (27:57-61)

Joseph of Arimathea is *a rich man*, says Matthew. In going to Pilate and asking for the body he is outing himself as someone *who had himself become a disciple of Jesus* (57).

Matthew may be encouraging us to do the same.

Joseph places Jesus *in his own new tomb that he had cut out of the rock* (59). After rolling a large stone over the entrance, he *went away* (60).

The job is done. End of story.

And, all the while, two of the women are there, still watching (see 61 and 55).

b. – The guards at the tomb (27:62-66)

The next day, *the chief priests and the Pharisees* go to Pilate to ask for a guard on the tomb (62). The reason is that they have heard that *that deceiver said, 'After three days I will rise again'* (63).

Their fear is that *his disciples may come and steal the body and tell the people that he has been raised from the dead* (64b).

The guard Pilate gives the Jewish leaders for the tomb is made up of some of his own soldiers, who will be answerable to him (see chapter 28:14a).

So, says Matthew, *they went and made the tomb secure* (66).

c. – The empty tomb and the risen Jesus (28:1-10)

Matthew doesn't describe Jesus' resurrection for us, but he does tell us two important things which point unmistakeably to it.

First, the tomb is empty (1-7). The two Marys go to the tomb (see 1, also chapter 27:55 and 61) and find that things have changed dramatically.

An angel, accompanied by an earthquake, has *rolled back the stone and sat on it* (2): *his appearance was like lightning, and his clothes were white as snow* (3). No wonder the guards are frightened out of their wits (see 4).

The angel shows the women that the tomb is empty: *He is not here; he has risen, just as he said* (6a). So he tells them to *come and see the place where he lay* (6b).

Now he gives them a job to do. They are to *go quickly and tell his disciples* that Jesus has risen from the dead and will meet them in Galilee (7, and see chapter 26:32).

The angel has passed on the message he was given by Jesus: *Now I have told you* (7b). And the women leave, *afraid yet filled with joy* (8).

Second, the women meet Jesus (8-10): *Suddenly Jesus met them* (9a). They experience the risen Jesus.

So *they came to him, clasped his feet and worshipped him* (9). And Jesus tells them to get on with the job of passing on his message to the disciples (see 10).

These are the two most important pieces of evidence for the resurrection of Jesus: his tomb was empty and his followers met him.

This should prompt *us* to worship Jesus, just as it did the women.

b'. – The guards' report (28:11-15)

Some of the guards *reported to the chief priests everything that had happened* (11). The response is to give the soldiers a bribe to enjoy (see 12)

Section Six: The Lover (Matthew 26:3 – 28:20)

and a story to tell: *His disciples came during the night and stole him away while we were asleep* (13).

The bribe is necessary because sleeping on guard duty was a punishable offence. The problem with the story, though, is that if they were asleep the soldiers could have no idea that it was the disciples who had removed the body!

The religious leaders who thought Jesus' disciples would not tell the truth (see chapter 27:64) are now resorting to deceit themselves.

Matthew tells us that *this story has been widely circulated among the Jews to this very day* (15).

a'. – Jesus: sovereign and sending (28:16-20)

The women have obviously passed on the message, because *the eleven disciples went to Galilee, to the mountain where Jesus had told them to go* (16).

When they see the risen Jesus, *they worshipped him; but some doubted* (17). Worship is the natural response when confronted with the reality of the resurrection; but doubt is understandable.

So Jesus comes closer and says these astonishing words: *All authority in heaven and on earth has been given to me* (18). The grammar means that *God* has given this to him.

The background of Jesus' words is, once again, Daniel's prophecy about the glorious Son of Man approaching the Ancient of Days. Daniel writes that *he was given authority* (Dan 7:14a); now Jesus is claiming that that is exactly what has happened.

On that basis (*Therefore,* 19a) the disciples are to *go and make disciples of all nations* (19a). This is astonishing.

The command earlier in the Gospel to proclaim the message of the kingdom of God only to Israel (see chapter 10:5-6, and see also my comments on chapter 15:24) is again shown to be temporary: *all nations* are to be told the good news about Jesus.

And the aim is not only that people hear the message, but that they also start *following* Jesus: the disciples are to *make disciples* (19).

In order to do this, the disciples need to do two things.

First, they are to baptise people (19). This will be a public act of allegiance and will be *in the name of the Father and of the Son and of the Holy Spirit* (19).

Jesus puts himself up there with the Father and the Spirit: he is to be worshipped as they are. But this is *one* God: the word *name* in verse 19 is singular.

This will remind us of Jesus' own baptism back in Section One of the Gospel: as John baptised Jesus, we *saw* the Spirit and we *heard* the Father (see chapter 3:16-17).

And second, the disciples are to teach people (20a). New disciples need to learn to *obey everything I have commanded you* (20a).

And so they need teaching. Following Jesus means obeying him, and that is only possible if we discover what he wants us to do.

So this teaching role of the disciples will be crucial.

Now Jesus promises that *I am with you always, to the very end of the age* (20b). Did the disciples understand this to be a reassurance that the Holy Spirit would constantly bring the presence of Jesus to them? Jesus had certainly promised this in the Upper Room (see John 14:16-18; 16:6).

At the beginning of the Gospel, we were told that Jesus is Immanuel, which means *God with us* (see chapter 1:23). Now, at its close, Jesus promises that his presence is always with those who follow him.

And this promise is not only for the eleven disciples *then*. It is also for us *now*: this is until *the very end of the age* (20b).

Teaching

What has happened to the teaching part of Section Six?

In this book I have taken the repeated phrase *When Jesus had finished...* as marking the end of each section (see chapter 7:28; 11:1; 13:53; 19:1; 26:1).

This means that each section consists of a narrative part, followed by a teaching part.

One reason many commentators don't like this Matthew structure is that chapter 26:3 – 28:20 doesn't have a teaching part or a *When Jesus had finished...* ending. The result, they say, is that there are really only five sections, with what I call Section Six being an epilogue.

But, of course, that's a problem. How can the account of the death and resurrection of Jesus be relegated to an epilogue?

So for this reason many commentaries opt for another Matthew structure (see Appendix 1, Question 2, for a little more on this).

Section Six: The Lover (Matthew 26:3 – 28:20)

But I want to defend the view that my Section Six is a genuine section. And there is a good reason for this.

The narrative part, as we have seen, runs from chapter 26:3 to chapter 28:20. But there *is* a teaching part too.

In the very last verse of the Gospel Jesus tells the disciples that, as they tell people his message, they are to be *teaching them to obey everything I have commanded you* (chapter 28:20).

Teaching. Now Jesus is passing on the responsibility for this task to the disciples.

So I think the structure of Section Six in the Gospel of Matthew looks like this:

Narrative (26:3 – 28:20)
Teaching (chapter 29)

The first verse of the book of Acts sheds interesting light on this. Luke, its author, says that his first book (which we know as Luke's Gospel) was about all that Jesus *began* to do and teach (Acts 1:1).

In other words: the book of Acts is going to tell us about what Jesus *continued* to do and teach – through the apostles and the church.

So in my view we are in the teaching part of Matthew's Section Six *now*, as the church commits itself to proclaim the good news about Jesus and to *make disciples of all nations* (see chapter 28:19).

And, all the while, Jesus is building his church (see chapter 16:18).

So I imagine that Matthew might like this sentence to describe the end of human history: *When Jesus had finished building his church, he came back in glory.*

With that, Section Seven will begin: after Judgment Day a new heaven and a new earth.

And that is a section which will *never* end!

Learning the Gospel

Please take time to learn Section Six: I'm sure that the early Christians did. It is not hard to do, as most of us are fairly familiar with the story.

Block A is easy to learn: it's short and it's a sandwich.

Then turn to Block B. Remember that the first incident (a) explains the last (a'): the last supper explains the crucifixion. Remember, too, that the events are in pairs, as follows:

The last supper leads into Jesus' prediction of Peter's denial.
His prayer in Gethsemane is followed by his arrest there.
While Jesus is before the high priest, Peter is denying his Lord.
The Roman governor hands Jesus over to be crucified by Roman soldiers.

After you have Block B lodged in your memory, it is time to turn to Block C. The mirror linking here makes this easy to learn.

I am praying that you will enjoy learning Section Six of Matthew's Gospel!

Section Six: The Lover
Narrative

A
- a. Plans against Jesus
- b. The anointing at Bethany
- a'. Plans against Jesus

B
- a. The last supper
- b. Jesus predicts Peter's denial

- c. Gethsemane
- d. Jesus arrested

- d'. Before the Jewish Council
- c'. Peter denies Jesus

- b'. Jesus before Pilate (and Judas hangs himself)
- a'. The crucifixion

C
- a. Jesus: dead and buried
- b. The guards at the tomb
- c. The empty tomb and the risen Jesus
- b'. The guards' report
- a'. Jesus: sovereign and sending

Teaching
Chapter 29

Meeting the Lord

As you move through the events of Section Six in your mind, or together with a friend, stop and thank Jesus for his love at every step of the way. Ask him to make these events real to you; ask him to touch your heart with his love.

Take time to worship him, too, as you recognise that he has conquered death. And commit yourself again to *make disciples*.

As you re-tell Matthew, you will rediscover Jesus.

My Conclusion: The Experiment goes on

I hope you have taken time on your way through *The Matthew Experiment* to learn the structure of the Gospel.

If you have, you have heard *Jesus the Teacher* telling disciples and would-be disciples what it means in practice to follow him; you have seen *Jesus the Lord* working miracles with effortless authority, before sending his disciples out to proclaim the kingdom of God; you have watched as he is increasingly seen as *Jesus the Enemy* by the religious authorities.

You have seen how he has revealed himself to his disciples as *Jesus the Son*, explained that he will suffer and die, and how he has committed himself to building his church; you have heard *Jesus the Judge* showing what life in the kingdom of God looks like and explaining how his judgment will be at work in the present, in the near future and at the end of human history; and you have seen the supreme self-sacrifice of *Jesus the Lover* as he goes to the cross to die for our sins.

You have seen his empty tomb with the two Marys and witnessed their encounter with the risen Jesus. And you have watched as he has sent out his disciples with the command to make disciples of all nations.

And, whether you have learnt and used the structure or not, I hope you have been rediscovering Jesus.

But that process doesn't need to stop because you have reached the end of this book. I want to suggest a few ways in which you can keep using Matthew's Gospel to help you get to know Jesus better.

1. Using Matthew's Gospel for worship and prayer

Take one section of Matthew. As you begin to run through it in your mind (without your Bible), don't just remember the order of the narrative and the teaching: talk to Jesus about what he is doing and saying. Enjoy spending time with him. Worship him for his power and his love. And pray for yourself as you think your way through the section.

You can do this at home in your room, or while you are sitting on the bus. You might decide to use Section One this way for a week; the following week you could move on to Section Two.

2. Using Matthew's Gospel to help you pray for others

Sometimes you want to pray for a friend or a family member, but you're not sure how. Why not take one section of the Gospel and pray through it, praying the whole time for this particular person?

With some incidents you will be praying that she will recognise more and more who Jesus is and why he came; sometimes you will be praying that the message of the cross will move her as never before; sometimes you will be praying that she will experience what it means to be sent out by Jesus to tell others his good news.

Matthew's Gospel can help you pray for others, whether these people are already Christians or not.

3. Using Matthew's Gospel for a Matthew Walk

Go for a walk (without a Bible) with a friend who has learnt the same section(s) of Matthew as you have. Take turns to tell each other the incidents and the teaching, including as many details as you can remember. This is not a competition: you can help one another as you re-tell Matthew.

When you get home you might take some time to thank Jesus and worship him together. (You might also want to turn to Matthew's Gospel to remind yourselves of any details neither of you could remember.)

The Matthew Walk works well with a group too. But however you do it, it is so healthy to be using Matthew's Gospel to help you get to know Jesus better!

4. Using Matthew's Gospel in a teaching programme

Your youth group or student group might decide to use the structure of Matthew in its term programme. At your first meeting you could look at Matthew's Introduction, at your second meeting Section One, and so on.

Obviously you won't be able to cover every detail. But different small groups could look at different parts of the section, before each group shares with everyone else what they've learnt.

And some of the small groups might decide to learn the structure of the week's section for themselves, so they can use it in the week to come.

This could work well, too, in a church's Sunday teaching programme. The first sermon in a series could be on chapters 1 and 2 (Matthew's Introduction). Then you could have one or two sermons on each section in turn.

Of course this will be more of an overview than a detailed study of every paragraph. But sometimes, in the longer Bible books where we often get lost, an overview is exactly what we need.

5. Using Matthew's Gospel in a home group

It is possible to study the whole of Matthew's Gospel – and to learn it too! – in a home group context. There are suggested outlines for such a series in Appendix 3.

Finally…

Thank you for reading *The Matthew Experiment*.

Being a Christian is about much more than just knowing lots about Jesus. Once we have turned from our sin and trusted him, it's about *encounter*: getting to know him better.

The Holy Spirit uses all kinds of things to help us to grow. But I am convinced of this: what he uses more than anything else to help us to know Jesus better is the Bible.

Please pray for yourself, and for others trying the Matthew experiment, that all of us will love and experience Jesus more.

This will make us want to help other people to become his disciples too (see chapter 28:18-20).

Appendix 1:
Questions about Matthew's Gospel

Below are some of the questions I have most often been asked about Matthew's Gospel. I can only comment briefly here: see the larger commentaries for more details.

1. Who says Matthew's Gospel has a structure at all?

I can't prove that it has, but it seems to me to make sense.

In a culture in which you couldn't print off copies of books, it strikes me that writing with a memorable structure is the obvious thing to do.

As Matthew was writing something he considered incredibly important, he wanted people to pass it on to others: if they could learn the order of everything off by heart, that's exactly what they could do.

2. What are the main views about Matthew's structure?

All of the commentaries note the refrain at the end of Matthew's longer teaching passages: *When Jesus had finished...*

But most scholars are unwilling to conclude that this repeated phrase provides us with a five- or six-section structure of Matthew. This is either because there is no *When Jesus had finished...* at the end of Section Six, or because they find it hard to identify a main theme for each of the resulting sections.

So most commentaries opt instead for a structure based on the phrase *From that time on...* which occurs in chapter 4:17 and in chapter 16:21. The result is a structure which looks like this:

The introduction to Jesus' work (1:1 – 4:16)
The development of Jesus' work (4:17 – 16:20)
The climax of Jesus' work (16:21 – 28:20)

My problem with such a structure is that the three sections are so long, that learning the order of the events will prove difficult, if not impossible.

But most commentaries settle on this structure or a variant of it: most of them don't consider my view about the value of *learnability* in the first century (see Question 1, above).

And perhaps they are right.

3. Isn't it a problem that each of my six sections has a different structure?

The first thing to say is that each section *does* have the pattern of a narrative part followed by a teaching part.

But it is true that each section is different from the others.

To my surprise, this has not presented a problem. I don't find myself confusing one section with another: the differences in the internal structure actually *help* me to memorise the material.

4. What is the relationship between Matthew's Gospel and Mark's Gospel?

The issue of the order in which the Gospels were written (known as the synoptic problem) is reckoned to be one of the most complicated in all literature: I make no claim to have studied this topic in detail.

The majority of scholars think the evidence suggests that Mark's Gospel was written first, and that Matthew used and expanded Mark.

That may well be the case. But it is worth mentioning that this is far from proven.

In the first few centuries of the church it was taken for granted that Matthew was the first Gospel to be written: indeed, this was the view held almost universally until the middle of the nineteenth century.

And there are some scholars today who still argue for that position.

For myself, I am agnostic on the issue. I have written *The Matthew Experiment* without a particular solution to the synoptic problem in mind.

5. What is my favourite commentary on Matthew?

While I have learnt from many Matthew commentaries, the one I am most impressed by and have used most is IVP's Tyndale New Testament Commentary by Dick France. He is always biblical, thorough and clear.

And I found his treatment of chapters 24 and 25 (in this commentary and in his longer one) especially enlightening and convincing.

R. T. France, *Matthew: An Introduction and Commentary*, InterVarsity Press 2008.

Appendix 2:
The Mirror Links in Section Six

As far as I can see, Matthew has included mirror links only in Section Six of his Gospel. Sometimes these links are more obvious, sometimes less so.

Most of Matthew's mirror links are to be found in Mark's Gospel, too. (For the relationship between Matthew's Gospel and Mark's, see Appendix 1, Question 4 and the longer commentaries.)

Sometimes these links point out similarities, and sometimes contrasts. But always they are a help for the memory.

You may not be convinced by all the links I suggest: I can live with that.

Section Six, Block A

a and a' Jesus' enemies plot against him.

Section Six, Block B

a and a' the last supper (a) explains the cross (a').

b and b' the disloyalty of the disciples (b) is contrasted with the loyalty and steadfastness of Jesus (b').

c and c' Jesus warns Peter of the dangers of prayerlessness (c); Peter demonstrates its results (c'). Jesus prays three times (c); Peter fails three times (c').

d and d' the disloyalty of the disciples (d) is again contrasted with Jesus' steadfastness under pressure (d').

Section Six, Block C

a and a' the contrast between Jesus dead (a) and Jesus risen (a').

b and b' the guard is set on the tomb (b); the story the guards tell to explain away the empty tomb (b').

Appendix 3:
The Matthew Experiment in a Home Group

The following series of studies has 8 sessions and is designed for group use; but of course you could also use these questions for your own study or one-to-one with a friend.

These studies are meant for people who have already read the relevant section in *The Matthew Experiment*. In a home group context it might make sense if everyone reads the whole section in Matthew's Gospel before coming to the meeting: this will save significant time.

One possible way of doing these studies in a group is to divide into pairs: each pair looks at one part of the passage and tries to answer the questions. After 10 minutes, each pair shares what they have learnt and the group talk about it.

It is up to you whether you combine answering the questions with learning the structure!

8 Weeks in Matthew's Gospel

Week One
Matthew's Introduction (Matthew chapters 1 and 2)

Look at chapter 1:1-17

1. What does this genealogy tell us about Jesus? Why are these things important?
2. Why do we think Matthew has written verse 16 so carefully?

Look at chapter 1:18-25

3. Matthew tells us three times that Jesus' birth is going to be supernatural: where in the passage does he do this?
4. How do we think Joseph felt in verse 19? And in verses 24 and 25? Why?

Look at chapter 2:1-12

5. The Magi were Gentiles. Why do we think they wanted to see the king of the Jews?
6. Why did they do the things Matthew tells us about in verse 11?

Appendix 3: The Matthew Experiment in a Home Group

Look at chapter 2:13-23

7. What shows us here that God wanted to protect Jesus? Why was this so important to him?

8. As we look back on these first two chapters of Matthew's Gospel, let's make a list together of some of the things we have learnt about Jesus.

Do any of us know the structure of Matthew's Introduction? Or would any of us like to?

Week Two
Section One: The Teacher (Matthew 3:1 – 7:29)

Look at chapters 3 and 4

1. Which do we think are the most important incidents in these two chapters? Why?

2. Baptism is for sinners. Why did Jesus insist on being baptised?

Look at chapters 5, 6 and 7

3. Chapter 5 is about the deeper righteousness Jesus is looking for in those who follow him. In what ways are disciples meant to be different from other people?

4. In chapter 5:17-48 Jesus highlights six areas of righteousness. Which of them do we find the most challenging?

5. In chapter 6:5-15 Jesus talks about prayer. What should all of us remember when we pray?

6. Why should none of us worry about material things? What is there about God which will help us not to worry?

7. Why do we need God's help not to judge others? How do we know God will help us?

8. What, according to Jesus, is the main thing that shows that someone is really his disciple? If we commit to living like this, what will be the result in our lives?

Do any of us know the structure of Section One? Or would any of us like to?

Week Three
Section Two: The Lord (Matthew 8:1 – 11:1)

Look at chapter 8:1-22

1. What do the leper, the centurion and Peter's mother-in-law have in common? Which of these three healings is the biggest surprise?

2. Do we think Jesus is a bit harsh with the two men who want to follow him in verses 18-22? What does he want to make clear about discipleship?

Look at chapter 8:23 – chapter 9:17

3. Of the three miracles here, which is the most extraordinary? Which tells us the most about Jesus?

4. Why do we think it was important to Matthew to tell us how he came to follow Jesus? In what ways does reading *his* story help *us*?

Look at chapter 9:18-38

5. Jesus gives life, opens eyes and loosens tongues. Let's share with one another how we have experienced Jesus doing that in our own lives.

6. Why did Jesus feel compassion when he saw the crowds at the end of the chapter? What did this make him do?

Look at chapter 10

7. How have we experienced opposition when we have tried to tell other people about Jesus? How did this make us feel?

8. Let's make a list of the things in this chapter that can help us not to give up when people are not interested in Jesus. What helps *you* the most?

Do any of us know the structure of Section Two? Or would any of us like to?

Week Four
Section Three: The Enemy (Matthew 11:2 – 13:53)

Look at chapter 11

1. What does Jesus say is the reason people will be condemned on the day of judgment?

2. What does Jesus say about himself in this chapter? What does he offer, and how can we receive it?

Look at chapter 12

3. Why do the religious leaders see Jesus as their enemy? What do they criticise him for?
4. What Old Testament passage does Matthew use to describe Jesus? How might we sum up its message for an eight-year-old?
5. Why do we think Jesus is not willing to give a sign to people who are determined to reject him?

Look at chapter 13:1-53

6. The parable of the sower teaches us that not everyone will respond positively to Jesus. Do we find this parable encouraging or discouraging?
7. Which of the other parables in this chapter do we think is the most important? Why?
8. What difference will it make to us if we listen to what Jesus is teaching in his parables?

Do any of us know the structure of Section Three? Or would any of us like to?

Week Five
Section Four: The Son (Matthew 13:54 – 19:2)

Look at chapter 13:54 – chapter 16:12

1. What are some of the things Jesus does in this part of Section Four which show that he is the Son of God? Which incident would have had the greatest impact on each of us?
2. What responses to Jesus here are surprising to us? And which do we find most challenging?

Look at chapter 16:13 – chapter 17:27

3. How do we think Jesus felt when Peter said chapter 16, verse 16? And how do we think Peter felt when Jesus said verses 17 and 18?
4. Is it good news or bad news for us that Jesus is building his church (see chapter 16:18)? Why?

5. In what way was Peter a stumbling-block to Jesus in chapter 16:23? Why do we think Jesus spoke so harshly to Peter?
6. What does the transfiguration tell us about Jesus? What impact do we think it had on Peter, James and John?

Look at chapter 18

7. How does Jesus say we should treat people in the Christian family who others might see as unimportant? How can we help one another do this?
8. What have we not understood if we refuse to forgive people who have sinned against us or hurt us in some way?

Do any of us know the structure of Section Four? Or would any of us like to?

Week Six
Section Five: The Judge (Matthew 19:3 – 26:2)

Look at chapter 19:3 – chapter 20:34

1. In chapter 19:3-26 Jesus talks about marriage, children and possessions. Which of these is the hardest issue for our culture? And which is the hardest for us in the church?
2. In chapter 19:27 – 20:16 Jesus talks about rewards for disciples. Which of the three matters most to you?
3. In chapter 20:17-34, how could we describe Jesus?

Look at chapter 21:1 – chapter 22:46

4. Where does Jesus talk about the importance of fruit here? Why is this a big deal?
5. Let's make a list of some of the lessons we can learn from the parable of the tenants.

Look at chapters 23, 24 and 25

6. What is Jesus' main criticism of the religious leaders in chapter 23? Why do we need to read this chapter carefully?
7. What do we think it means to be ready to welcome Jesus when he comes back in glory? In what way do the three parables in chapter 24:45 – chapter 25:30 motivate us to be ready?

8. How will Jesus make his decisions on Judgment Day? What will he be looking for in our lives? How might this impact us now?

Do any of us know the structure of Section Five? Or would any of us like to?

Week Seven
Section Six: The Lover (Matthew 26:3 – 28:20)

Look at chapter 26:3-56

1. Let's make a list of all the ways Jesus shows his love to others. Why is this extraordinary?
2. In what ways do the disciples let Jesus down in this part of the section?

Look at chapter 26:57 – chapter 27:26

3. Where do we see in this passage that Jesus is determined to go to the cross?
4. Peter and Judas both fail Jesus. What is the difference between them? What can we learn from this?

Look at chapter 27:27-66

5. When do we think Jesus was suffering most as he hung on the cross?
6. What is there here which shows that Jesus' death was actually a victory? How does this make us feel?

Look at chapter 28

7. What are the two pieces of evidence Matthew gives us so that we can believe Jesus rose from the dead?
8. Why is it important for us to know that Jesus possesses *all authority in heaven and on earth* (see verse 18)?

Do any of us know the order of the events in Section Six? Or would any of us like to?

Week Eight
Review of Matthew's Gospel

1. Let's all take 3 minutes to look through the Gospel and pick moments which are highlights for us. Then share in the whole group.

2. Why does Andrew suggest in *The Matthew Experiment* that we are all in the teaching part of Section Six? Do we think this is a bit far-fetched?

3. Why might you invite a younger Christian to read through Matthew's Gospel with you?

4. And why might you invite a friend who is not a Christian to read through Matthew's Gospel with you?

5. Let's keep our Bibles open as we pray together. Let's thank God for as many things in Matthew's Gospel as we can think of, and ask him to help us to be faithful followers of Jesus.

Do any of us know the structure of Matthew's Gospel? Or would we like to?

Appendix 4:
The Structure of Matthew's Gospel

Matthew's Introduction (Matthew 1:1 – 2:23)

A. **Jesus: the climax of history (1:1-17)**
   1. He's the son of Abraham (1-2)
   2. He's the son of David (1-17)
   3. He's the Jewish Messiah (1,16,17)

B. **Jesus: a supernatural birth (1:18-25)**
   1. Matthew says it (18)
   2. The angel says it (19-21)
   3. Scripture says it (22-23)

C. **Jesus: worshipped by Gentiles (2:1-12)**
   1. They follow a star (1-2)
   2. They learn from Scripture (3-8)
   3. They worship Jesus (9-12)

D. **Jesus: protected by God (2:13-23)**
   1. The first dream (13-18)
   2. The second dream (19-22a)
   3. The third dream (22b-23)

Section One: The Teacher (Matthew 3:1 – 7:29)

Narrative (3:1 – 4:25)

A. **His forerunner (3:1-12)**
   1. John's message (1-6)
   2. John's warning (7-10)
   3. John's master (11-12)

B. **His baptism (3:13-17)**
   1. John's objection (14)
   2. Jesus' explanation (15)
   3. God's proclamation (16-17)

C. **His temptation (4:1-11)**
   1. 'Turn these stones into bread' (3-4)
   2. 'Throw yourself down from the temple' (5-7)
   3. 'Worship me, and I'll give you the world' (8-19)

D. His message (4:12=17)
1. When Jesus preaches it (12)
2. Where Jesus preaches it (13)
3. Why Jesus preaches it (14-16)

E. His team (4:18-22)
1. His initiative (18-19, 21)
2. His promise (19b)
3. His attractiveness (20, 22)

F. His agenda (4:23-25)
1. Proclaiming the kingdom (23a)
2. Many miracles (23b-24)
3. Large crowds (25)

Teaching (5:1 – 7:29)

A. Our character (5:3-12)
1. Our relationship to God (3-6)
2. Our relationship to others (7-12)
3. The rewards Jesus promises (3-12)

B. Our task (5:13-16)
1. The salt of the earth (13)
2. The light of the world (14-16)

C. Our righteousness (5:17-48)
1. Murder (21-26)
2. Adultery (27-30)
3. Divorce (31-32)
4. Oaths (33-37)
5. Retaliation (38-42)
6. Hatred (43-47)

D. Our devotion (6:1-18)
1. Giving (2-4)
2. Praying (5-15)
3. Fasting (16-18)

E. Our ambitions (6:19-34)
1. Wanting stuff (19-24)
2. Worrying about stuff (25-34)

Appendix 4: The Structure of Matthew's Gospel

F. Our relationships (7:1-12)
 1. Don't judge others (1-5)
 2. Don't batter hard hearts (6)
 3. Ask God for help (7-11)

G. Our Jesus-centredness (7:13-27)
 1. The gate and the road (13-14)
 2. The tree and its fruit (15-23)
 3. The wise and foolish builders (24-27)

When Jesus had finished... (7:28-29)

Section Two: The Lord (Matthew 8:1 – 11:1)

Narrative (8:1 – 9:38)

A. Who Jesus loves (8:1-17)
 1. He heals a leper (1-4)
 2. He heals a centurion's servant (5-13)
 3. He heals Peter's mother-in-law (14-15)

B. Two warnings for disciples (8:18-22)
 1. A man who claims too much (18-20)
 2. A man who offers too little (21-22)

C. Where Jesus is Lord (8:23 – 9:8)
 1. He rules nature (23-27)
 2. He crushes evil (28-34)
 3. He forgives sin (9:1-8)

D. Two stories for disciples (9:9-17)
 1. Jesus calls Matthew and eats with sinners (9-13)
 2. Jesus predicts a radical break with Judaism (14-17)

E. What Jesus does (9:18-34)
 1. He gives life (18-26)
 2. He opens eyes (27-31)
 3. He loosens tongues (32-34)

F. Two facts for disciples (9:35-38)
 1. What Jesus feels (35-36)
 2. What Jesus wants (37-38)

Teaching (10:1 – 11:1)

A. Mission: its authority (10:1-4)
1. Where it's from (1)
2. Who it's for (2-4)

B. Mission: its description (10:5-15)
1. Proclamation to Jews, not Gentiles (5-6)
2. Proclamation in word and deed (7-8)
3. Proclamation while trusting God (9-15)

C. Mission: its opposition (10:16-25)
1. Arrest and trial (16-20)
2. Betrayal and hatred (21-23)
3. Being treated like Jesus (24-25)

D. Mission: its secret (10:26-42)
1. There is a Judgment Day (26-33)
2. This is part of the plan (34-36)
3. There are two responses (37-42)

When Jesus had finished... (11:1)

Section Three: The Enemy (Matthew 11:2 – 13:53)

Narrative (11:2 – 12:50)

A. Three questions (11:1-19)
1. A question about Jesus (1-6)
2. A question about John (7-15)
3. A question about the crowds (16-19)

B. Jesus: his message (11:20-30)
1. Condemnation: a warning of judgment (20-24)
2. Invitation: an offer of rest (25-30)

C. Three attacks (12:1-50)
1. 'He's breaking the Sabbath' (1-21)
2. 'He's working with Satan' (22-37)
3. 'He should give us a sign' (38-45)

Teaching (13:1-53)

A. First parable: The sower (13:1-23)
1. The puzzle (3-9)
2. The reason (10-17)
3. The solution (18-23)

B. Three parables about growth (13:24-43)
1. The weeds (24-30)
2. The mustard seed (31-32)
3. The yeast (33-35)
4. The explanation of the parable for the weeds (36-43)

C. Three parables about response (13:44-50)
1. The treasure (44)
2. The pearl (45-46)
3. The net (47-48)
4. The explanation of the parable of the net (49-50)

D. Last parable: The householder (13:51-52)

When Jesus had finished... (13:53)

Section Four: The Son (Matthew 13:54 – 19:2)

Narrative (13:54 – 17:27)

A. Jesus: the authority he demonstrates (13:54 – 14:36)
1. Opposition in Nazareth (13:54-58)
2. The death of John the Baptist (14:1-12)
3. Feeding of the 5,000 (14:13-21)
4. Jesus walks on the water (14:22-33)
5. Healings in Gennesaret (14:34-36)

B. A double warning for disciples (15:1-20)
1. God's word and human tradition (1-9)
2. What makes people unclean? (10-20)

C. Jesus: the responses he gets (15:21 – 16:12)
1. Jesus and the Canaanite woman (15:21-28)
2. Jesus heals many Gentiles (15:29-31)
3. Feeding of the 4,000 (15:32-39)
4. The Pharisees and the Sadducees demand a sign (16:1-4)
5. The confusion of the disciples (16:5-12)

D. A double revelation for disciples (16:13-23)
   1. Peter's confession of Jesus (13-20)
   2. Jesus' first prediction (21-23)

E. Jesus: the disciples he wants (16:24 – 17:27)
   1. The call to discipleship (16:24-28)
   2. The transfiguration (17:1-13)
   3. Jesus drives out an evil spirit (17:14-21)
   4. Jesus' second prediction (17:22-23)
   5. Paying the temple tax (17:24-27)

Teaching (18:1 – 19:2)

A. Be small (18:1-5)
   1. Becoming like a little child (2-4)
   2. Welcoming a little child (5)

B. Be careful (18:6-9)
   1. Causing others to stumble (6-7)
   2. Causing myself to stumble (8-9)

C. Be caring (18:10-14)
   1. Respecting little ones (10)
   2. Rescuing little ones (12-14)

D. Be discreet (18:15-20)
   1. Step One (15)
   2. Step Two (16)
   3. Step Three (17-20)

E. Be forgiving (18:21-35)
   1. Peter's question (21-22)
   2. Jesus' parable (23-34)
   3. Our responsibility (35)

When Jesus had finished... (19:1-2)

Section Five: The Judge (Matthew 19:3 – 26:2)

Narrative (19:3 – 22:46)

A. Three issues Jesus addresses (19:3-26)
   1. Marriage (3-12)

Appendix 4: The Structure of Matthew's Gospel   183

    2. Children (13-15)
    3. Possessions (16-26)

B. Three rewards Jesus promises (19:27 – 20:16)
    1. Disciples will share his victory (28)
    2. Disciples will gain more than they give up (29)
    3. Disciples will experience the surprises of the new age (19:30 – 20:16)

C. Three things Jesus does *before* entering Jerusalem (20:17-34)
    1. Jesus' third prediction (17-19)
    2. The Zebedee family request (20-28)
    3. The healing of two blind men (29-34)

D. Jesus enters Jerusalem (21:1-11)
    1. What Jesus does (1-7)
    2. What the crowds shout (8-9)
    3. What everyone asks (10-11)

E. Three things Jesus does *after* entering Jerusalem (21:12-27)
    1. He clears the temple (12-17)
    2. He curses the fig-tree (18-22)
    3. He confuses the religious leaders (23-27)

F. Three parables Jesus tells (21:28 – 22:14)
    1. The two sons (28-32)
    2. The tenants (33-46)
    3. The wedding banquet (22:1-14)

G. Three traps Jesus avoids (22:15-46)
    1. Paying taxes to Caesar (15-22)
    2. Marriage at the resurrection (23-33)
    3. The greatest commandment (34-40)

Teaching (23:1 – 26:2)

A. Judgment on the scribes and the Pharisees (23:1-39)
    1. Warning about the scribes and the Pharisees (1-12)
    2. Condemnation of the scribes and the Pharisees (13-36)
    3. Bad news for the scribes and the Pharisees (37-39)

B. Judgment in the fall of Jerusalem (24:1-35)
    1. The end is not yet (4-8)
    2. How to live in the meantime (9-14)

3. How to recognise the Judean crisis (15-28)
4. The temple's destruction and the Son's triumph (29-31)
5. Jesus' final answer to the disciples' first question (32-36)

C. **Judgment at the return of Jesus (24:36 – 25:46)**
1. His coming: unpredictable and inescapable (24:36-44)
2. Our readiness (24:45 – 25:30)
   a. the parable of the servant put in charge (24:45-51)
   b. the parable of the girls waiting for the bridegroom (25:1-13)
   c. the parable of the servants given lots of money (25:14-30)
3. His judgment: final and authoritative (25:31-46)

When Jesus had finished... (26:1-2)

Section Six: The Lover (Matthew 26:3 – 28:20)

Narrative (26:3 – 28:20)

Block A (26:1-16)
a. Plans against Jesus (1-5)
b. The anointing in Bethany (6-13)
a'. Plans against Jesus (14-16)

Block B (26:17 – 27:56)
a. The last supper (26:17-30)
b. Jesus predicts Peter's denial (26:31-35)
c. Gethsemane (26:36-46)
d. Jesus arrested (26:47-56)
d'. Before the Jewish Council (26:57-68)
c'. Peter denies Jesus (26:69-75)
b'. Jesus before Pilate (and Judas hangs himself) (27:1-26)
a'. The crucifixion (27:27-56)

Block C (27:57 – 28:20)
a. Jesus: dead and buried (27:57-61)
b. The guards at the tomb (27:62-66)
c. The empty tomb and the risen Jesus (28:1-10)
b'. The guards' report (28:11-15)
a'. Jesus: sovereign and sending (28:16-20)

Teaching (chapter 29)

How to Teach the Bible so that People Meet God

Andrew Page

Andrew Page believes that Bible teaching can be a supernatural event. A graduate of London School of Theology, Andrew was a missionary in Austria for 20 years, working with the Austrian Christian student movement (IFES) and later pastoring a church in Innsbruck.

He says "Two enemies of Christian churches are Bible teaching with little biblical content and Bible teaching which is more a lecture than an event." If you agree with this, *How to Teach the Bible so that People Meet God* is the book for you.

This is unashamedly a how-to book. Andrew has trained others in this method of teaching a Bible passage in a number of countries around Europe, and now for the first time the method is available as a book.

So, 3 questions before you buy this book:
- Do you want to find out if God has given you the gift of teaching?
- Do you want to grow in the gift you believe you have?
- Do you want to help a friend to develop as a Bible teacher?

If you have said *Yes* to any of these questions, *How to Teach the Bible so that People Meet God* is a great place to start.

ISBN 978-3-95776-035-7
Pb. • 64 pp. • £ 7.50

VTR Publications
info@vtr-online.com
http://www.vtr-online.com

The 5 Habits of Deeply Contented People

Andrew Page

Have you found contentment?
Most people are looking for it.
If you're not, it may be because you've given up...

If you are searching or want to start your search again, *The 5 Habits of Deeply Contented People* is the book for you.

The Bible says that everyone is made in God's image. Andrew Page says there are 5 habits which express that image of God in us. He says "If we can work out what these habits mean in practice for us as individuals, we will experience a deeper level of contentment."

Basing what he writes on the second chapter of the Bible, and making clear that these habits work even if we don't believe in God, Andrew invites his readers to try out the habits for themselves.

- Do you want to be more contented, whatever life throws at you?
- Are you curious to know what it means to be made in God's image?
- Would you like to find out if the 5 habits work?

If you have said Yes to any of these questions, *The 5 Habits of Deeply Contented People* is a great place to start.

ISBN 978-3-95776-009-8
Pb. • 52 pp. • £ 7.00

VTR Publications
info@vtr-online.com
http://www.vtr-online.com

The John Experiment

How John's Gospel can help you know Jesus better

Andrew Page

Are you looking for a new way into the Gospels? Whether you have been a Christian for many years or are just considering the Christian faith, John's Gospel is a great place to start.

In The John Experiment Andrew Page unpacks John's Gospel and shows you how to commit it to memory. He explains how learning to meditate on the Gospel events is transforming his relationship with Jesus.

Would you like to give it a go? If your answer is Yes, then The John Experiment is the book for you.

ISBN 978-3-95776-070-8
Pb. • 146 pp. • £ 9.50

VTR Publications
info@vtr-online.com
http://www.vtr-online.com

The Mark Experiment

How Mark's Gospel can help you know Jesus better

Andrew Page

If you are looking for a new way into Mark's Gospel and you long to allow the Gospel to help you worship and experience Jesus, *The Mark Experiment* is the book for you.

In *The Mark Experiment* Andrew Page shows you how to commit the Gospel to memory and explains how learning to meditate on the Gospel events has transformed his relationship with Jesus. Think what this might mean for your understanding of the life and ministry of Jesus.

One exciting result of this book has been the development of an innovative drama in which a team of 15 Christians from a church or student group acts out every incident in the Gospel of Mark as theatre-in-the-round. The Mark Drama is now being performed in many countries around the world.

www.themarkdrama.com

ISBN 978-3-937965-21-5
Pb. • 106 pp. • £ 8.00

VTR Publications
info@vtr-online.com
http://www.vtr-online.com